W9-BDY-445

How to Live with a **NUT ALLERGY**

How to Live with a **NUT ALLERGY**

Everything You Need to Know if You Are Allergic to Peanuts or Tree Nuts

CHAD OH, M.D.

CHIEF OF ALLERGY/IMMUNOLOGY, HARBOR-UCLA MEDICAL CENTER AND ASSOCIATE PROFESSOR, UCLA SCHOOL OF MEDICINE

AND CAROL KENNEDY

McGraw·Hill

New York   Chicago   San Francisco   Lisbon   London   Madrid   Mexico City
Milan   New Delhi   San Juan   Seoul   Singapore   Sydney   Toronto

HOWARD COUNTY LIBRARY
BIG SPRING, TEXAS

The McGraw·Hill Companies

Library of Congress Cataloging-in-Publication Data

Oh, Chad K.
    How to live with a nut allergy / by Chad K. Oh and Carol Kennedy. — 1st
ed.
        p.   cm.
    ISBN 0-07-143002-4
    1. Food allergy—Popular works.   2. Nuts—Popular works.   I.
Kennedy, Carol.   II. Title.

    RC596.04   2005
    616.97'5—dc22   2004005355

Copyright © 2005 by Chad K. Oh and Carol Kennedy. All rights reserved. Printed in
the United States of America. Except as permitted under the United States
Copyright Act of 1976, no part of this publication may be reproduced or
distributed in any form or by any means, or stored in a database or retrieval
system, without the prior written permission of the publisher.

1 2 3 4 5 6 7 8 9 0   DOC/DOC   3 2 1 0 9 8 7 6 5 4

ISBN 0-07-143002-4

McGraw-Hill books are available at special quantity discounts to use as premiums
and sales promotions, or for use in corporate training programs. For more
information, please write to the Director of Special Sales, Professional Publishing,
McGraw-Hill, Two Penn Plaza, New York, NY 10121-2298. Or contact your local
bookstore.

This book is printed on acid-free paper.

To my wife and children: Michelle, Brian, Kristina, and Sarah
To my parents, Jinwoo and Soonbok Oh
To my parents-in-law, Eungyu and Inkyu Lee

—Chad Oh, M.D.

Contents

Part II
What to Do About Nut
and Peanut Allergies

Acknowledgments

The creation of a book involves the help and guidance of a wide range of individuals and experts. Thanks to Angelika Koerner, Sharon Crain, Bob Crain, and Marijeke Coudenys. Also thanks to the Allergy and Asthma Network; the American Academy of Allergy, Asthma, and Immunology; the American Academy of Pediatrics; the American College of Allergy, Asthma, and Immunology; the American Peanut Council; Anaphylaxis Canada; the Asthma and Allergy Foundation of America; the Food Allergy and Anaphylaxis Network; the National Institute of Allergy and Infectious Disease; and the MedicAlert Foundation.

Thanks also to Barbara Gilson; Ellen Vinz; my agent, Gene Brissie, at James Peter Associates; and Michael and Kara.

Introduction

Peanut and nut allergies are the leading cause of fatal and near-fatal food-induced anaphylaxis in the United States. In fact, peanut allergies in children have increased twofold over a five-year period from 1997 to 2002, according to a study in the *Journal of Allergy and Clinical Immunology (JACI)*. And yet as serious as this allergy can be, only a small number of people carry injectable epinephrine (EpiPen), and only 74 percent of children and 44 percent of adults with more severe reactions seek medical evaluation. Each year in the United States, thousands of people rush to hospital emergency rooms, and about fifty to one hundred people die, after accidentally eating peanuts or tree nuts.

Currently, the best way to prevent these emergencies is to educate people about how to avoid eating foods containing peanuts and nuts, and how to self-administer EpiPens after an accidental ingestion. (An EpiPen is a preloaded syringe that injects a single dose of epinephrine for the emergency treatment of severe allergic reactions.)

For more than ten years, I have been taking care of patients with peanut and nut allergies as a pediatric allergist and immunologist, while conducting basic research on allergic inflammation—a major mechanism of peanut allergy. In my practice, I have seen a wide range of patients who experienced everything from mild skin rashes to significant systematic anaphylactic symptoms after eating peanuts or tree nuts. In this book, I include some of my clinical cases to help you understand the clinical characteristics, diagnosis, and management of peanut and tree nut allergies.

Peanuts and tree nuts are an inexpensive source of dietary protein predominantly eaten in peanut butter and snack nuts—and unfortunately, they have become some of the world's most allergenic foods. More and more nuts are finding their way into food products either directly or by indirect contamination of food products during the manufacturing process. Nuts and peanuts may masquerade on a food label as anything from "hydrolyzed vegetable protein" to "groundnuts," and it's important to realize that for the sensitive person, this lifelong allergy can be fatal in even trace amounts.

Despite the widespread seriousness of the problem, far too many people don't really understand these allergies. I hope that this book will provide the information that parents and adult patients are looking for, together with the very latest research on prevention and cause of these allergies, including the newest research about potential new treatments.

In my current position as chief of allergy and immunology at Harbor-UCLA Medical Center in Torrance, California, and associate professor at the UCLA School of Medicine, I see many of the problems that a peanut or nut allergy can cause. Living with such an allergy can be quite a challenge, and the more information people have at their fingertips, the easier their lives can be.

It's almost impossible to find a book about both peanut and nut allergies for the general reader, but from the number of our patients, I knew there was a need for this information. So this book is for you— the allergic individual—and your family, as a way of addressing all of the issues you face. In this book you'll find a basic description of peanut and nut allergies—what they are, how they begin, and how they affect your body. You'll learn who treats peanut and nut allergies and what kinds of tests to expect, how to handle and operate an EpiPen, and what to do in case of a severe allergic reaction.

The book also discusses how to handle a variety of situations that may confront a person with a nut or peanut allergy—how to handle a variety of travel situations, how to help your allergic child have a safe school experience, what to look out for when eating out in restaurants, and much more. We conclude the book by taking a quick look at upcoming research and potential treatment breakthroughs.

These are exciting times to be working in the field of immunology, as scientists home in on possible vaccines and treatments that we hope will make fatal nut reactions a thing of the past. Major breakthroughs in the prevention and treatment of severe peanut and tree nut allergies are bringing hope to the three million Americans suffering from the condition. It is for these patients that we wrote this book.

Part I

All About Nut and Peanut Allergy

Nut and Peanut Allergies: What's It All About?

Jim B. was a busy young stockbroker who stopped by the mall on his way home to grab a chocolate chip cookie at a nationally known cookie store. Because he was highly allergic to nuts and peanuts, he told the clerk he wanted a cookie "without nuts." Assuming Jim didn't like nuts, the clerk handed over a peanut butter chocolate chip cookie. Almost instantly, Jim's throat swelled shut. Within moments, a full-scale emergency resuscitation was underway. Jim left the cookie store with a breathing tube in his trachea, but thankfully, a quick response from emergency personnel made the difference between life and death for Jim. Others aren't always so lucky.

More than three million Americans, like Jim, have an allergy to tree nuts or peanuts—and the numbers are increasing every year. Ironically, nuts and peanuts—the most popular, most readily available dietary proteins—cause some of the most pervasive and severe allergies.

Peanut allergy is probably the most common cause of death by food anaphylaxis in the United States. Every year, about one hundred allergic Americans actually die after eating nuts or peanuts. Typically, most people with other types of food allergies develop and then eventually lose their sensitivity to the food. But while very young children allergic to milk proteins, soy, or eggs tend to lose their allergies as they grow older, about 80 percent of children with nut and peanut allergies remain allergic to these foods for life.

As I explain to my patients, unlike with other food allergies, it only takes very small amounts of peanuts or nuts to trigger a reaction. This is why nut and peanut allergies are so serious—patients with severe reactions react to lower doses of an allergen (a substance that causes an allergy). People with nut or peanut allergies can be so sensitive that they can have an anaphylactic reaction if they kiss someone who has recently eaten a nut or peanut, or if they eat with a utensil that touched a peanut or nut. Others who are severely nut allergic can have a reaction after simply inhaling the aerosolized allergen in the odor or fragrance of nuts or peanuts.

What Is a Nut Allergy?

Allergies to nuts and peanuts often begin during the first years of life and account for severe and potentially fatal reactions. Because nuts and peanuts are so common and are often hidden ingredients in other foods, it's hard to avoid them—and accidental ingestions with severe reactions are common.

This is exactly what happened to my eight-year-old patient "Stacy," who had been diagnosed with a peanut allergy at age two. Her mother was very careful to monitor what she ate, and she had been doing fine—until she went to a birthday party with her mother and ate a sugar cookie. Within minutes, she developed a severe reaction and was rushed to the emergency room, where she was admitted for a few days. Her mother told me she'd checked to make sure there was no trace of peanuts in the sugar cookie. Most likely, the sugar cookie had been lying beside— or had touched—a peanut butter cookie. This shows that you can't be too careful when dealing with peanut allergies. This is why I strongly recommend that patients and their caregivers always carry an EpiPen.

In some ways a nut allergy is like any other allergy—an exaggeration of the body's natural immune defenses that are designed to recognize harmful substances in your blood or organs. An allergic reaction occurs when your body's immune system wrongly perceives an allergen as a threat. Nut or peanut allergens are proteins that can still cause reactions even after they are cooked or have been digested in the intestines.

When the nut or peanut allergen enters your body, the immune system "sensitizes" the body by producing immunoglobulin E (IgE) antibodies that recognize peanut or nut allergens. These IgE antibodies probably evolved initially to conquer parasites that entered the body. In people with a nut or peanut allergy, however, these antibodies treat nuts or peanuts as the enemy. For an allergic reaction to happen, your body must thus first become sensitized to the nut or peanut allergen. One or more encounters with the allergen programs your immune system to recognize it and react aggressively, because your immune system now mistakenly believes that the nut or peanut is actually harmful. Once your body has been sensitized to nut or peanut allergens, when you next eat a nut or peanut (or food that contains nuts or peanuts) your immune system unleashes an army of chemicals to protect the body that affect the respiratory system, gastrointestinal tract, skin, or cardiovascular system.

Your immune system does this by sending IgE antibodies that activate a type of immune cell called a mast cell, which releases histamines and many other chemicals that affect your eyes, nose, throat, lungs, skin, or gastrointestinal tract, causing the symptoms of the allergic reaction. Mast cells are found in all tissues of the body. Depending on their location, they can cause a wide variety of responses. For example, mast cells that are activated on the skin can cause hives, redness, or itchiness. Mast cells in the digestive tract can trigger vomiting or diarrhea. In the throat, mast cells can be involved in closing off the airways; this can ultimately be fatal. People with peanut or nut allergy have high levels of IgE that recognize peanut or nut allergens and stimulate an exaggerated immune response.

Interestingly, your immune system is capable of learning, which means that each time in the future that you are exposed to nuts or peanuts, your immune system will act more quickly, triggering an allergic reaction that may become even worse with each subsequent exposure.

Nut allergies differ from most other allergic reactions and present specific challenges. Nuts are one of a small group of foods that can trigger anaphylaxis, the most severe form of allergic reaction, which is potentially life-threatening. Yet a nut or peanut allergy is also notoriously unpredictable, so that the patient may not always have the same kind of allergic reaction each time a nut or peanut is eaten. Even individuals who have only ever suffered mild symptoms after exposure to nuts may in the future be at risk of suffering a severe anaphylactic reaction to nuts. Peanuts and nuts also can cause a severe reaction in very small amounts.

Recent evidence indicates that even trace amounts of these foods can be enough to cause a major reaction in those individuals who are severely allergic.

Peanuts are a complex plant food, with more than thirty different proteins. Research is under way to identify exactly which proteins trigger an allergic reaction and why the reaction can vary in severity among allergy sufferers.

Although the vast majority of reactions to nuts are not fatal, stories of people who died from nut or peanut allergy show that this can happen even to someone who has only had mild reactions before. To be safe, I regard these allergies as dangerous even if a patient has never had a serious reaction in the past.

After adolescence, the risk of having a reaction in any one year seems to drop for most people, but if you are having a serious anaphylactic reaction, the risk of dying from it seems to increase with age. This is probably because an older person's heart and blood vessels can't cope with such a reaction (or the epinephrine used to treat a reaction) nearly so well as a young person's organs.

Peanuts Versus Nuts

Although many people think peanuts are a type of nut, they're really a legume (*Arachis hypogaea* L.). Peanuts aren't true nuts, because they grow underground.

Technically, a peanut is a groundnut and belongs to the biological family Leguminosae (legumes), which includes peas, beans, lentils, and licorice.

Tree nuts are just what the name implies: nuts that grow on trees. They include hazelnuts (filberts), pistachios, Brazil nuts, cashew nuts, macadamias, chestnuts, almonds, pecans, and walnuts. While they are all tree nuts, different nuts can belong to different biological families; for example, pecans and walnuts belong to the Judanglacea family, almonds are of the Drupacea family (also including peaches, apricots, plums, nectarines, and cherries), and cashews and pistachios belong to the Anacardiaceae family, which also includes mangos.

However, the allergic reactions in people who are sensitive to peanuts are exactly the same as the reactions in those allergic to tree nuts; moreover, half of those individuals who are allergic to peanuts are also allergic to tree nuts, such as almonds, walnuts, pecans, cashews, and often sunflower and sesame seeds.

In some food groups (especially tree nuts and seafood), an allergy to one member of the food family may mean that the person is allergic to all the members of the same group. This is known as cross-reactivity. However, some people may be allergic to both peanuts and walnuts, which are from different food families; these allergies are called coincidental allergies, because they are not related.

Symptoms

As we've learned, peanut and nut allergies tend to trigger more severe symptoms than other food allergies and are characterized by a wide range of symptoms with even the slightest exposure. People who are allergic to nuts and peanuts often notice the effect in seconds, and their life may be in jeopardy within a few minutes. Sometimes a reaction takes much longer to start—up to an hour or so—but even so, it can still be extremely serious.

However, people allergic to nuts or peanuts may not all have the same type of reactions. Indeed, one person's symptoms may differ from one experience to the next. The intensity of a given anaphylactic attack is unpredictable because it depends on the amount of allergen contained in the food eaten and how sensitive the person is to the allergen. Some people may not even recognize that they are having a mild allergic reaction (it may be confused with symptoms of an environmental allergy or a cold). Others experience the life-threatening symptoms of anaphylaxis, which include breathing problems due to swelling of the throat or airways in the lungs, a severe drop in blood pressure, and sometimes loss of consciousness.

The first signs of an allergic reaction are often a runny nose, an itchy skin rash, or a tingly feeling in the mouth. With nut and peanut allergies, these mild symptoms can quickly become more serious. Nut and peanut allergies can be fatal if the immune response triggers immediate swelling that spreads to the vocal cords in a reaction called *laryngospasm*. Once the vocal cords swell shut, a person won't be able to breathe, and death can occur quite quickly.

A second type of fatal reaction is called *anaphylactic shock*, which is a body-wide allergic reaction that can be fatal. In this scenario, the allergic individual swallows and digests the nuts. Symptoms can appear either immediately or a few hours later, as the person begins to feel warm and flushed, followed by a tingling sensation in the mouth or a red, itchy rash. Some people develop hives around their mouth; others have hives all over their body. Other symptoms may include lightheadedness, shortness of breath, severe sneezing, anxiety, cramps, vomiting, or diarrhea. In severe cases, patients experience severe swelling in the upper airway tissues that obstructs breathing. As the lower airways constrict, shortness of breath, wheezing, or asthma may begin. In some very severe cases, fluid leaks from blood vessels into the tissues, leading to a drop in blood pressure that may result in a loss of consciousness and shock. Such severe reactions tend to occur within minutes after exposure and can be truly explosive.

As we described above, anaphylaxis may range from a mild reaction (with a skin rash or hives) that can be treated simply with antihistamines to severe or fatal reactions requiring an EpiPen injection, antihistamines, steroids, and emergency medical care.

Fortunately, the annual incidence of anaphylactic reactions is small—only about 30 out of every 100,000 people. People with asthma, eczema, or hay fever are at higher risk. Unfortunately, it's impossible to predict which allergic individuals will have a mild reaction and which will have a much more severe experience. In fact, reactions to eating peanuts are quite often severe—even the first time. Forty percent of first reactions to a peanut or tree nut allergy involve breathing problems.

You're at increased risk for a severe reaction if you have a combination of three factors: a peanut or tree nut allergy, a history of anaphylaxis, and asthma. High-risk people should always have two EpiPens handy, in case one misfires or you need a second injection; one dose only lasts about half an hour.

Causes of Nut and Peanut Allergies

In the last ten to twenty years, there has been a dramatic increase in the number of all types of allergic disorders, including nut and peanut allergies, but no one is sure whether the increased reports of nut and peanut allergies are due to an actual rise in incidence, or simply because patients and their doctors are just more aware of the problem.

There have been many different theories as to what could trigger the development of a nut or peanut allergy in a young child—everything ranging from early exposure to genetics. (You'll read about some of these in greater detail in the next chapter.) Some experts believe that the increase in reactions is related to the fact that mothers are eating more peanuts during pregnancy, thus sensitizing their unborn babies. Others think it's because young children are given peanut butter sandwiches or crackers as "quick meal substitutes" too early in life, before their immune systems have had a chance to develop.

Early Exposure

In recent years, we have come to believe that exposure to peanuts during the first few years of life—including prenatal exposure of babies whose mothers eat peanut or nut products—might help trigger allergies to nuts or peanuts. If that theory is right, delaying the introduction of these foods might prevent the allergy. We do know that with other types of allergies small children who are exposed to a potent allergen seem to be more likely to react.

Since the development of nut and peanut allergies has increased among young children, it's obvious that something has changed, and one of a number of things that have changed is diet.

Although allergies can develop at any age, there are only a few adults who have been eating nuts or peanuts all their lives and suddenly develop a sensitivity.

Genetics

Genetic factors are certainly linked to the development of other allergies, and the tendency to develop a nut or peanut allergy may be inherited. Typically, people who are allergic to nuts or peanuts come from families with lots of different types of allergies. We've known for a very long time that if one parent is allergic, there's a good chance the child will also be allergic; if both parents are allergic, the chance that their child will have the same problem is even higher.

A recent study of twins supports the idea that a nut or peanut allergy may develop not from early exposure to nuts or peanuts but from inheritance. In this research, scientists discovered that genetics accounts for about 80 percent of the risk of peanut allergy. This study, published in the July 2000 issue of the *Journal of Allergy and Clinical Immunology*, recruited pairs of twins in which at least one member had a peanut allergy. The fifty-eight pairs of twins included fourteen identical pairs and forty-four fraternal pairs. Among them were seventy people who had a history of peanut allergies, experiencing such symptoms as hives, wheezing, repetitive coughing, vomiting, or diarrhea within an hour of eating peanuts. About 65 percent of the identical twins shared an allergy to peanuts, compared to just 7 percent of the fraternal twins (the same rate found among siblings who are not twins). Of course, this 7 percent rate is still fourteen times higher than the risk of peanut allergy in the general population.

However, food allergies are probably not directly inherited. Disentangling the link between genes and the development of allergic antibody responses can be quite a complex endeavor. For example, the tendency (called *atopy*) to form allergic antibodies is inherited— more often from the mother. An atopic child exposed to peanut butter is at much higher risk of developing a peanut allergy than a normal child. Atopic children also tend to have other common allergic diseases, such as eczema, allergic asthma, and rhinitis. This could mean that an atopic child may not directly inherit a peanut or nut allergy, but simply the overall tendency to form antibodies.

Roasting

Another factor linked to peanut allergies is the fact that peanuts in Western countries (where the allergy is most common) are almost always eaten after they have been roasted. For some reason, roasting peanuts seems to increase their allergenicity.

In the Next Chapter

Now that you've learned what causes nut and peanut allergies, in the next chapter we'll discuss who is most at risk for developing these sensitivities.

2

Who's at Risk?

A few moments after enjoying her first taste of peanut butter, eight-month-old Kara K. began to cry as a white lesion appeared on her lip. Within moments, her face began to swell. In a few more minutes she was on her way to the emergency room, where she was treated for a life-threatening bout of anaphylaxis.

Unbeknownst to her parents, Kara was allergic to peanuts.

Doctors today agree that all types of allergies, including nut and peanut allergies, are becoming more common than ever before. When it comes to nuts and peanuts, most people develop the allergy in childhood—some as early as infancy. Unfortunately, we don't yet have a foolproof way of predicting who will develop such sensitivity to nuts, although scientists do have some clues.

Genetics

Although anyone can develop an allergy to peanuts or tree nuts (or both), the tendency toward allergic reactions is largely inherited. For example, those most likely to be counted among the three million Americans allergic to nuts or peanuts are young children, and those whose close family members have a range of allergies have an increased risk for developing sensitivity to nuts or peanuts. But other reports also suggest that in a few rare cases, it's possible to develop such an allergy after an organ transplant from a donor who was allergic.

Where there is a history of allergies such as asthma or eczema, children are two to four times more likely to develop an allergy as compared to children from families without allergic parents. And infants born to families with at least one parent or sibling with a personal history of hay fever, asthma, food allergy, or eczema may have a 20 percent chance of developing food allergies in the first five to seven years of life. In fact, if your brother or sister has a nut or peanut allergy, you're more likely to be allergic than if one of your parents has the sensitivity, since all types of allergy become more common in successive generations.

Food allergy is less common in families without such a personal history. Researchers found that peanut allergy is more common among brothers and sisters of those who are allergic to peanuts (7 percent) than in the parents or the general population (1.3 percent).

Prenatal Sensitization

It's quite possible that an initial sensitization to peanuts or nuts may occur during pregnancy, when a tiny amount of nut protein crosses the placenta—although there is as yet no definitive evidence to prove this. Several studies have suggested that in those families with a history of allergies, it might be a good idea for a woman to avoid nuts and peanuts during pregnancy, since it appears that these allergens can cross the placental barrier. It could be that the rising prevalence of nut and peanut allergies may reflect a general increase of atopy, which is inherited more often from the mother.

For this reason, I would advise women with an allergic condition (or who know that there is one in the family) to avoid peanuts and tree nuts while they are pregnant. This would apply to you if you, your baby's father, or one of your previous children has an allergic condition, or has had an allergic reaction to anything. Allergic conditions include eczema, asthma, hay fever, and any allergic response (such as a rash or itch) after eating other foods, such as strawberries or shellfish.

And remember, if you decide to avoid peanuts while you're pregnant or breastfeeding, you need to avoid not only natural peanuts or nuts, but also products that may contain them. These include peanut butter, cereals, cakes, biscuits, some salad dressings, some ice cream, and some breads. When eating in a restaurant, either ask if peanuts have been included or choose a simple meal which contains no "hidden" ingredients.

Age

Age is an important risk factor. Nut and peanut allergies are appearing at earlier and earlier ages—often within the first two years of a child's life. This is not surprising, since children under the age of three are most likely to be sensitive to nuts or peanuts because their immune systems cannot yet tolerate a wide range of new substances.

Newborns

Once your baby is born, you'll need to continue to be vigilant if there is any reason to suspect allergies in your family. Breastfeeding gives your baby protection against many infections; exclusive breastfeeding for the first six months of your baby's life helps decrease the risk of allergies in the early years of life. However, if you eat peanuts or tree nuts while you are breastfeeding, there is a small chance that your baby will come into contact with traces of peanut through your milk—especially if your baby is at high risk for developing allergies.

Although breastfeeding is recommended by the American Academy of Pediatrics for the first six months of a baby's life, a recent study published by the *Journal of the American Medical Association* found that peanut proteins are secreted into breast milk. In fact, they can be detected several hours after you've eaten nuts or peanuts. This might be enough to sensitize a baby already at risk for developing nut or peanut allergies, triggering the infant's immune system to manufacture allergic antibodies. For this reason, the American Academy of Pediatrics recommends that nursing mothers not eat peanuts or tree nuts while nursing. I agree that all high-risk breastfeeding patients should eliminate peanut and nut products from their diets.

Infancy

When an infant's immature immune system creates IgE antibodies to nuts or peanuts the first time the food is eaten, a food allergy is born. The next time the nut or peanut is eaten, the infant may experience symptoms of a food allergy. Because infants are especially vulnerable for developing food allergies, this is why allergy prevention should begin even before birth.

Some experts believe that peanut or nut allergies are increasing during infancy because parents are introducing peanut butter products too early. As a result, the American Academy of Pediatrics recommends that solid foods not be introduced in infants at risk for allergies until six months of age, and that parents of infants at increased risk for developing peanut or nut allergy eliminate all peanut products from the child's diet for at least the first three years.

Allergy Testing in Infancy

In addition, children under three years of age who are being evaluated for other allergies should be tested for peanut allergy, and any child with peanut- or tree-nut–specific IgE antibodies should avoid all peanut and nut products for three to five years. If no reactions to inadvertent ingestions have occurred in the interim, the child should be reevaluated for evidence of peanut and nut-specific IgE antibodies and clinical reactivity to peanuts.

Although youngsters are more likely to develop peanut or nut allergies, children up to age twelve seem to have a much lower risk of dying than do teenagers and adults, even if they experience anaphylaxis.

Adolescence

The biggest risk period for dying of nut or peanut allergies seems to occur during the teens and young adulthood, perhaps because young people of this age become more independent, are no longer protected so much by their parents, and may not be so careful to keep their rescue epinephrine with them constantly.

In fact, a recent survey of teens and preteens with food allergies and their parents indicates that social issues affect how young people manage their illness as they approach young adulthood. The findings revealed that 94 percent of teens consider social isolation the worst part about having food allergies—unlike their parents, who were more concerned about issues such as death.

Research shows that most fatalities due to food allergy occur between the ages of ten and nineteen during the transition from childhood to young adulthood, as the teen becomes more independent. Parents, teachers, friends, and health-care providers need to be aware that adolescents are at the highest risk of death from a food-induced allergic reaction. Education about risk-taking behaviors and the importance of emergency therapy are crucial in this age group. The gap between the parents' safety concerns and the teens' social concerns can only be breached when families talk about these issues and decide together how to manage them.

Seniors

Although it appears that the risk of accidentally eating nuts lessens as adults get older and adopt a less risky lifestyle, those older people who do experience anaphylaxis are more likely to die of it. Experts suspect this is probably because heart disease and hardening of the arteries, which are common in senior citizens, make older patients less able to withstand the physical stress of anaphylaxis or the drugs used to treat anaphylaxis.

Other Allergies

People who are allergic to nuts or peanuts and also have other allergies are at increased risk for a stronger-than-average reaction to nuts or peanuts. For example, if you have asthma or atopic dermatitis as well as nut or peanut allergies, you're at higher risk for severe anaphylaxis, since asthma tends to worsen anaphylaxis. People with asthma who get anaphylaxis need to be particularly careful to use preventive drugs for their asthma to cut this risk.

Outgrowing Peanut Allergy

Some of my patients do seem to outgrow peanut allergies. Twelve-year-old Matthew had an anaphylactic reaction to peanuts when he was three years old. Since then, he had avoided peanuts, until one day when he accidentally ate a chocolate bar containing peanut butter. He had forgotten his EpiPen, so his mother—thinking he was about to develop a severe allergic reaction—rushed him to the nearest emergency room. Surprisingly, he didn't experience any symptoms of a reaction—no fainting, no skin rash—even more than an hour after eating the peanut butter. Finally, he was sent home, and he never developed any symptoms of peanut allergy after eating the peanut butter. What does this tell us? That some people do actually "outgrow" peanut allergy—and that's been shown in recent studies.

While about 20 percent of children with peanut allergies will outgrow this sensitivity, about 50 percent of children with a history of peanut allergy *and* low blood levels of peanut IgE antibodies may be able to outgrow the problem. The problem is, it's not always easy to figure out which allergic children are going to outgrow their nut or peanut sensitivity and which won't.

Fortunately, in a 2003 Johns Hopkins study, researchers discovered that a common test measuring IgE antibodies can help pinpoint those most likely to outgrow the allergy. In the study, researchers tested eighty children with diagnosed peanut allergy who had IgE levels of five kilounits per liter or lower. After eating a small amount of peanuts in a challenge test, researchers recorded any reactions and discovered that 55 percent passed the test, indicating they were no longer allergic. About 63 percent of children with an even lower IgE level (less than two kilounits per liter) had also outgrown the allergy.

The Hopkins researchers also asked previous study participants who had passed a peanut challenge test to answer a survey on peanut consumption. About one-third continued to avoid peanuts, and two girls had a reaction to peanuts although they had passed the challenge before.

The researchers recommended that carefully controlled challenge tests be tried periodically on children aged four and older who have IgE levels of two kilounits per liter or less. Discovering that a child no longer is allergic can be helpful because it removes the tremendous burden of avoiding peanuts.

Peanut Allergies Can Resurface

But the news isn't all good. Even as scientists learned that some children can outgrow their peanut allergy, another surprising study revealed that peanut allergies that appeared to fade away in some of these children can actually *resurface* later on.

Researchers at the Mount Sinai School of Medicine in New York City have reported three children in whom peanut allergies disappeared and then later returned. All three were boys who first developed peanut allergies between a year and eighteen months of age. Their peanut allergies disappeared, but then returned when the boys were between six and ten years of age. Remarkably, when their allergy returned, the boys turned out to be *more* allergic than they had been before.

These findings, which were published in the November 7, 2002, issue of the *New England Journal of Medicine*, demonstrate that allergists who find that peanut allergies have subsided in their patients should not necessarily recommend that they can resume eating food containing peanuts or nuts.

Nut and Peanut Allergies After Transplants

Adding to the debate about peanut allergies that come and go is the new problem of developing such an allergy after an organ transplant. Rarely, it may be possible to transplant not just a person's organs, but also his or her IgE antibodies, leading to a transplanted allergy to nuts or peanuts.

According to a report in the January 27, 2003, issue of *Archives of Internal Medicine*, a sixty-year-old Australian transplant patient who had never experienced a nut allergy suffered an anaphylactic reaction from eating cashews a day after he returned home from the hospital. The fifteen-year-old liver donor had a history of nut allergy—and had, in fact, died from an anaphylactic reaction to peanuts. After recovering from the anaphylactic reaction, the transplant patient reacted positively to a skin prick test for peanuts, cashew nuts, and sesame seeds. The donor also had had specific IgE antibodies for these same three foods.

Doctors suspect that because the donor died of anaphylaxis, his liver probably contained IgE antibodies that were transferred to the new owner. The transplant patient experienced a second anaphylactic reaction eight months after the first incident, when he ate peanut-contaminated food.

Researchers conclude that organ donors may need to be screened for allergies to prevent IgE antibodies from being transferred with the transplant organs. Organ recipients should also be aware of the potential danger.

In the Next Chapter

Knowing who's at risk for developing a nut or peanut allergy is an important first step in protecting against severe reactions. Anyone who is suspected of having such an allergy should visit an allergist for a diagnosis; in the next chapter we'll discuss this first visit and explain the tests that are performed.

3

Diagnosing Nut and Peanut Allergies

Nut and peanut allergies are unpredictable, and reactions can vary from relatively mild to life-threatening. Therefore, if you or someone in your family have suffered an allergic reaction to nuts or peanuts—or if you even have reason to suspect such an allergy—I recommend that you visit a board-certified allergist for testing and diagnosis immediately.

Sometimes patients ask me: Do I really need to see an allergist to manage my allergy? The answer is *yes*. Once you've been diagnosed with a peanut or nut allergy, your care should be managed by an allergist. Well-trained allergists can discuss potential cross-reactions with other foods, and provide instruction for the prevention and emergency care—including how to use an EpiPen.

Finding an Allergist

So as you can see, an allergist is the best-qualified professional to diagnose a nut or peanut allergy, even if you're pretty sure you have had a serious reaction. Diagnosis requires a carefully organized and detailed assessment of the problem, using a thorough medical and dietary history, skin or blood tests, and occasionally, performing a food challenge.

If your insurance allows you to choose an allergist, you should try to locate one close to your home, since you will probably be visiting the office fairly often— at least at first. You can also look in the Yellow Pages of your phone book under "Physicians" with a specialty area of "Allergy and Immunology." You also can write, call, or visit the websites of the following organizations to obtain the names of board-certified allergists in your area:

American Academy of Allergy, Asthma and Immunology
611 East Wells Street
Milwaukee, WI 53202
(800) 822-2762
Website: www.aaaai.org

American College of Allergy, Asthma and Immunology
85 W. Algonquin Road, Suite 550
Arlington Heights, IL 60005

847-427-1200
Website: http://allergy.mcg.edu

Next, you'll want to check out the allergist's background: Is the person board-certified, personable, and experienced? Board certification is important because that guarantees that the physician has completed required immunology and allergy training.

What Is a Board-Certified Allergist?

A board-certified allergist is a physician who has undergone three years of training in either internal medicine or pediatrics, followed by another two or three years in the field of allergy and clinical immunology. The allergist must pass the board exams in either internal medicine or pediatrics before being allowed to take the allergy board exam given by the American Board of Allergy and Immunology. Once certified, the allergist must be reexamined every ten years to renew the allergy certification.

Take a list of questions or concerns to your first visit. You should feel comfortable in sharing your questions and concerns. The allergist should listen carefully to you, clearly answer any questions, and help you understand your nut or peanut allergy. If you're the parent of an allergic child, watch the interaction between them; make sure the doctor can relate to your child.

Medical and Dietary History

The best tool your allergist has to diagnose a food allergy is a good medical history. It can be difficult to isolate a range of vague or conflicting symptoms, but a good doctor is trained to sort through your descriptions of the sequence of the reactions and the timing of the symptoms.

The allergist will ask you about the frequency, seasonality, severity, and type of symptoms. He or she might ask about the amount of time between eating a food and any reaction. The allergist will ask you about your personal habits (such as smoking or drinking) and lots of questions about your environment. Since a true food allergy exists in only between 2 and 10 percent of cases, there could well be another cause for your symptoms.

Your allergist will also ask you detailed questions about any symptoms that you think are related to the nut or peanut allergy, and you'll be asked to describe exactly what happens:

- Do they involve your eyes, nose, and throat only?
- Is there itching, breathing problems, or coughing?
- How long do the symptoms last?
- When do the symptoms stop and start?

Types of Tests

There's no perfect way to measure your potential for a severe allergic reaction. Your allergist will take a detailed history of previous reactions and other allergic conditions you may have, and then recommend skin or blood tests to make an accurate diagnosis.

You also may be asked to keep a food diary to help pinpoint the problem. A food diary is a detailed record of the date and time that all food has been eaten, along with a description of type and timing of any symptoms. In addition to the food itself, you'll need to include all of the ingredients—there are often hidden ingredients you may not realize until you check out the box or bag. You'll also need to write down how much of the foods you eat.

When an allergy to one type of nut or peanut is suspected, your allergist may recommend eliminating the food for a time. If symptoms improve, the allergist may add the food to your diet once again to fur-

ther determine if it causes a reaction. This is never recommended for people with a history of anaphylaxis,
however.

Next, it may be time for a skin or blood test to zero
in on exactly what type of nuts will trigger a response
(some people are allergic to all kinds of nuts, while
others have a problem with just a few types). This is
especially important in young children, whose immature immune systems means that an allergy to one nut
puts them at high risk of developing allergies to others.

There are several different methods for testing for
nut and peanut allergies, and both skin tests and blood
tests (RAST tests) are used in testing for food allergies.

Skin Tests

Skin-prick tests (also called prick-puncture tests) are
the most commonly used assessments for nut and
peanut allergies. Intradermal tests can be used if the
skin-prick test results are inconclusive. These tests are
usually done on your back or forearm, where a number of different allergens can be assessed at the same
time.

In each test, the allergist creates a solution containing an extract of the suspected peanut or tree nut
allergen. In a skin test, when the allergen solution
comes in contact with any IgE antibodies, it triggers
a reaction that leaves a mark on the skin.

However, skin tests are far from perfect—as many as 50 percent of patients who react to a skin test for nuts or peanuts do not have any allergy symptoms when they eat these nuts, indicating that a false positive reaction has occurred. However, a false negative reaction occurs in only a few percent of patients with nut or peanut allergies. Therefore, a positive skin test means that you may need further tests to confirm the results, whereas if the test is negative it's very likely that you don't have an allergy to these allergens.

Control Tests Because each person's skin can react in a unique way, the allergist must first determine a way to tell the difference between skin irritation and a true allergic response. The typical way to do this is to begin with a negative and positive control test.

In the negative control test, the allergist administers a tiny drop of diluent solution on the skin. No response to the diluent solution is expected, so if you react to the solution, it suggests that your skin is highly sensitive and might well have a false positive reaction to the real allergen skin test.

In a positive control test, the allergist applies a histamine solution to your skin, which should always trigger a response. If you don't respond to the histamine, it could be that you're taking medication that is blocking the response; this could also block the reaction to allergens, giving a false negative result. For this reason, doctors advise their patients not to take antihistamines, cough medicines, and certain antidepressants three to six days before the tests are done.

The results of these two control tests are compared with the other skin tests using a millimeter ruler, from side to side and top to bottom. If the reaction to one of the nut or peanut allergens is equal to or larger than the reaction from the histamine (positive control) test, your response is said to be "positive." If the skin reaction from the allergen is equal to or smaller than the diluent test (the negative control test), then your reaction is "negative." If the reaction is more than the diluent but less than the histamine, it's up to the allergist to interpret the results.

While skin tests are fairly straightforward, their results can be influenced by a wide variety of individual characteristics, including your age, existing medical conditions, or current medications, as well as the season of the year and the part of the body where the tests are performed.

Skin reactions will be smaller in infants and older people. If you have eczema, diabetes, or cancer, or you are having regular hemodialysis, you may have a milder reaction to the allergen tests.

Certain medications—especially antihistamines—will affect the skin tests. Your allergist may ask you not to take any antihistamines between one day and two months before the test (depending on the strength of the antihistamine). Other medications, including tri-

> **Caution!**
>
> If you have had an anaphylactic reaction to peanuts or tree nuts, you should not undergo allergy skin testing with peanut or tree nut allergens. Even a tiny amount of nut allergen could trigger a severe reaction.

cyclic antidepressants, anti-nausea drugs, some asthma drugs, and the antihistamine drug ketotifen, can all affect test results.

The testing site also can affect the type of reaction to the skin test. Areas on the back are more reactive than the forearm, and the middle and upper back are more reactive than the lower back; the area just below the bend in your arm is more reactive than your wrist.

Finally, the season of the year in which the test is performed can affect results if you are also allergic to pollen. Stronger skin test reactions occur during and just after the pollen season.

Skin-Prick Testing A skin-prick test is probably the most commonly used method of allergy testing and is suitable testing for nut and peanut allergies. The tests are easy to administer and almost completely painless. One advantage of the skin-prick test is that as many as seventy to eighty allergens can be assessed during the same appointment, and results are available immediately. A "positive" result will be visible within fifteen to twenty minutes.

In the test, the allergist cleans your skin and then places a small drop of the suspected allergen on the skin, followed by a prick with a device so that some of the solution moves just under the skin. After about fifteen minutes, the skin is dried and inspected. In the case of nut allergy, the appearance of a blister in the center of a red, swollen patch will indicate that an allergy to the particular nut is present. The doctor will measure the size of the welt, which is usually between three to five millimeters in diameter.

The "scratch test" is a variation of the skin-prick test. In this version, the skin is first scratched; the allergen is then placed on the spot. This version is considered to be less accurate than the skin-prick test.

Skin-prick testing is considered to be a safe way to test for nut allergy, since only a tiny drop of the allergen is administered. However, it's still very important that a qualified allergist perform the test in a place where expert medical attention is available if needed. It's also important to remember that skin-prick tests are not always accurate, and they aren't recommended if you have a history of anaphylaxis.

Intradermal Test If the results of the skin-prick or scratch test are inconclusive, the allergist may consider an *intradermal test*. In this assessment, a tiny amount of the suspected nut or peanut allergen is injected into your skin with a very fine needle. Because the intradermal tests use a higher concentration of allergen, they are considered to be more accurate. However, this also means they are more likely to trigger adverse reactions, and also generate more false positives than the skin-prick test. This test is not recommended if you have a history of anaphylaxis.

Blood Tests

In some cases, blood testing may be considered more appropriate, although these tests are more expensive without being more accurate. They're usually chosen for anyone who has previously experienced an anaphylactic reaction, or if skin-prick testing may be impractical because the patient suffers from widespread eczema.

Here's an example about why a blood test may be a safer way to assess allergies: Ten-year-old John had asthma, and had avoided eating peanuts because of a high-risk family history for peanut allergy. When he accidentally ate a peanut butter cookie one day, within two hours he developed lip swelling, coughing and wheezing, abdominal cramps, and voice changes. He was treated in the emergency room, but when skin tests were performed in a local clinic later, they elicited a very strong reaction, including severe skin rashes and shortness of breath. As this case shows, it would have been better to have used blood tests with John; blood tests are a safer way to test for peanut allergy if a peanut allergy is strongly suspected.

I also recommend blood tests for patients who can't safely stop taking antihistamines, cough medicines, and some antidepressants, which they would need to do in order to have a skin-prick test. Also, blood tests are a good idea for those people whose skin is so sensitive that it reacts to everything (a condition known as *dermatographism*).

RAST (radioallergosorbent test) is the most common type of blood test to determine nut or peanut allergy. In this procedure, the allergist measures the presence of IgE antibodies that relate to a particular allergen in the blood by taking a small amount of blood from a vein in the arm. The results are graded from zero to six—the higher the grade, the more likely the person is allergic to that substance. Test results are usually available within seven to fourteen days.

Unfortunately, RAST results are not always conclusive—a negative test does not mean that the person is absolutely not allergic to nuts or peanuts. On the other hand, some allergy sufferers who have stopped experiencing symptoms or have outgrown their allergy will have a positive RAST.

There's no direct link between the level of your IgE antibodies and the severity of future allergic reactions. This is particularly important when testing for nut allergies, since the severity of the reaction is highly

Unconventional Allergy Tests

The following alternative, nonconventional allergy tests are currently used, but are not recognized by conventional medical practitioners.

- **Hair analysis.** In this test, a sample of a person's hair is sent to a lab for a measurement of its mineral content, which is supposed to reveal allergies by measuring toxic levels of heavy metals or low levels of selenium, zinc, chromium, manganese, and magnesium. However, research studies failed to show any diagnostic value. Although experts concede hair analysis may have some value as a screening device for heavy metal exposure, it is not reliable for evaluating a patient's allergy status.

   Experts note that a wide variety of substances (including shampoo, bleaches, and dyes) can affect the hair's mineral content. And because the hair grows so slowly, even hair closest to the scalp is several weeks old, which means it may not reflect the current health status of an individual anyway.

A study published in the January 3, 2001, issue of the *Journal of the American Medical Association* concluded that hair mineral analysis was unreliable, and noted that problems with regulation and certification should also be assessed.

- **Leukocytotoxic tests.** White blood cells are mixed with the suspected allergen and observed under a microscope. The theory goes that if an allergic patient's white blood cells are mixed with the nut allergen, they will swell. The test measures any swelling of the white blood cells, which would indicate a positive result. Despite claims to the contrary, no large studies have ever shown the test to be accurate in the forty-four years it has been available.

- **Neutralization-provocation testing.** A specific dose of neutralized allergen drops are placed under the tongue. Experts have shown, however, that patients cannot distinguish test extracts from placebo controls by this procedure, so the basis of a positive test is merely the power of suggestion. This procedure is therefore not helpful in diagnosis and treatment.

unpredictable and can vary greatly from one reaction to the next. You should interpret results with caution.

Allergy tests are an important way to detect suspected allergies, but test results should always be interpreted by a qualified medical doctor. The results on their own aren't conclusive and should be assessed in the context of your specific medical history. Factors such as family history of allergies or the patient's history of eczema and asthma provide vital clues in the overall picture of the patient's condition.

Food Challenge

If the results of the skin or blood tests are unclear, the allergist may opt to perform a food challenge. During this test, you might be given gradually increasing amounts of nuts or peanuts to eat, while a doctor watches for symptoms. This can only be performed in a hospital, where access to immediate medical care and medications are available. It should never be performed if you have experienced a clear-cut anaphylactic reaction to nuts or peanuts in the past.

In the Next Chapter

Now that you've learned how nut and peanut allergies are diagnosed, in the next chapter we'll discuss how to treat reactions that occur when the person comes in contact with nuts or peanuts.

Allergic Children

Experts suggest that children under age three who are being tested for other allergies also should be tested for peanut allergy even if there is no history of anaphylactic reaction to peanuts. Any child with peanut-specific IgE antibodies should avoid all peanut and nut products for three to five years. If no reactions to accidental exposure to nut or peanut products have occurred during that time, the child should be reevaluated for evidence of peanut- and nut-specific IgE antibodies.

Part II

What to Do About Nut and Peanut Allergies

4

Treating Nut and Peanut Allergic Reactions

Of course, it's best to be able to prevent an accidental exposure to nuts or peanuts (you'll learn more about that in Chapter 5). But once you've been exposed to a nut or peanut, it's important to take the right steps to treat the reaction.

As we discussed earlier, a severe reaction doesn't always occur—some people only experience mild anaphylaxis, with itching, hives, or skin redness. In this case, you can simply use a fast-acting antihistamine (such as Benadryl) to treat symptoms. Benadryl is the most well known, since it's very effective and works quite quickly (usually within an hour). Even pregnant women and young children can safely use this medication, although it causes sleepiness. Benadryl is used during an acute allergy reaction because it works faster (fifteen minutes) than non-sedating antihistamines such as Claritin (which takes forty-five to sixty minutes). Injection of the liquid forms of antihistamines are preferable, since they enter the bloodstream more quickly than tablets do.

If you have asthma in addition to nut or peanut allergies and you experience wheezing when you are exposed to an allergen, you'll need a bronchodilator to help open up your narrowed breathing passages in addition to the Benadryl. But people with food allergies who don't have asthma probably won't need to carry inhalers.

Injected epinephrine (the EpiPen) is the drug of choice for severe anaphylaxis. But it's important to remember that an injection of epinephrine doesn't *cure* the allergic reaction—it only eases the immediate effects so you can seek emergency medical care. With proper medical attention and treatment, food allergies are rarely fatal.

Here's how epinephrine works: During anaphylaxis, your blood vessels leak, breathing passages swell, and blood pressure drops, causing choking and collapse. Injected epinephrine acts quickly to constrict blood vessels, relax smooth muscles in the lungs to ease breathing, stimulate the heartbeat, and help to stop swelling around the face and lips. It also works to ease an acute asthma attack caused by a food allergy.

Symptoms of anaphylaxis can be quickly reversed by injecting epinephrine, followed by antihistamines and other emergency measures. And because the effects of epinephrine quickly wear off, you may need a second injection if you're having a very severe reaction.

It is essential that anyone with severe anaphylaxis get emergency treatment immediately. This is particularly important since up to 40 percent of people who have a severe reaction to nuts or peanuts have a second attack (called *biphasic anaphylaxis*) in which symptoms return from one to four hours after the first reaction. This reaction does not respond to antihistamines, and steroids may not be effective either. That's why medical treatment in an emergency room is so important after a severe reaction.

What Is an EpiPen?

The EpiPen is a device containing a premeasured amount of epinephrine delivered by a small ½-inch needle. The injection is not very painful, and the shot can provide immediate relief of the symptoms of an allergic reaction. If you or a family member has a severe nut or peanut allergy, you should always have an EpiPen within reach so that if an anaphylactic reaction occurs, you can administer epinephrine to help counteract it. It's a good idea to keep several EpiPens available at all times—for home, school or work, in the car, and so on. Remember that if you're at risk for a severe reaction, you should have two EpiPens available in case you need a second dose.

Learning How to Use an EpiPen

Your doctor should have given you instructions on how to use the EpiPen, but easy-to-follow instructions are also printed right on the device. When your doctor first prescribes an EpiPen for an allergic member of your family, read the instructions included in each package immediately so you'll be familiar with them before an emergency occurs.

Many people—especially children and teens—are uncomfortable with the idea of giving a shot, and worry about whether they will be able to inject themselves in case of an allergic reaction. Doctors often suggest that people who are uncertain about using an EpiPen practice with an EpiPen Trainer. These training devices are reusable and don't contain a needle or medicine. The more a patient practices giving an injection, the easier it will be to do so in an emergency.

You also can practice using the EpiPen by injecting an expired pen into an orange or a grapefruit. Experts say that practicing on fruit can give a person a good idea of the amount of pressure that is needed to activate an EpiPen. Because quick treatment is important during a nut or peanut allergic response, the EpiPen is designed to work through clothing.

Studies have shown that a delay in receiving epinephrine is most often the cause of fatal anaphylaxis. If you or someone in your family is worried that you won't know how to administer medication, talk to your doctor.

Carry Your Own EpiPen!

Many states don't allow emergency medical technicians (EMTs) to carry epinephrine. Find out if your state does; if not, be sure to always have your own EpiPen with you!

First Steps in Treating Anaphylaxis

If a nut-sensitive person begins to feel faint after eating nuts or peanuts, have the person lie down. However, if there is swelling in the throat with difficulty in breathing and there is not a serious problem with faintness, it is better to have the patient sit up to avoid making the throat swelling worse. If the patient is feeling faint and has throat swelling, you'll need to decide which is most life-threatening. In any case, you'll need to get help quickly. The next step is to decide whether or not you need to inject epinephrine.

To Inject or Not to Inject?

Many patients and families worry about knowing when to use an EpiPen. At the beginning of an anaphylactic reaction, it is impossible to tell how severe the reaction is going to be. Many experts believe it's better to treat all cases of anaphylaxis early rather than to try giving treatment too late. You should certainly not wait until you (or your nut-allergic child) are beginning to suffer severe problems in breathing before injecting epinephrine.

Most experts believe that the earlier you give the treatment, the better it works, especially since rapid progression of symptoms is a danger sign. Moreover, just because previous anaphylactic reactions may have been mild does not guarantee that a life-threatening reaction will not occur sometime in the future. Although it's true that most sufferers who have had mild attacks in the past do seem to have relatively mild repeat attacks, some people have died from an unexpected severe reaction after having a history of only mild attacks in the past.

If the person with an allergy gets just a few itchy, swollen spots near the lips and the reaction doesn't seem to be getting worse, the doctor may simply recommend keeping the EpiPen nearby and monitoring the person's condition, being prepared to inject quickly if the person's condition deteriorates. In any case, you need to discuss with your doctor the right time to administer the injection.

You should probably give an injection if any of these signs of a serious reaction are present:

- Marked difficulty in breathing or swallowing
- Sudden weakness
- Steady deterioration

If you're in doubt, most experts would recommend that you administer epinephrine. If you think there may be any risk to life because of difficulty in breathing or because the person is beginning to feel faint, then the earlier you give the epinephrine the better it will work.

How to Administer

Remember that non-medically trained people should only inject epinephrine into the muscle of the outer thigh—nowhere else.

1. Form a fist around the auto-injector with the black tip facing down. Pull off the gray activation cap. Do not remove the activation cap until you are ready to use the auto-injector. Once the activation cap is removed,

the auto-injector is ready for use and can be activated. Never put your fingers over the black tip when removing the activation cap or after the activation cap has been removed.

2. Place the black tip against your outer thigh. (You don't have to remove your clothing.) Do not put your thumb over the end of the unit.

3. With a quick motion, push the auto-injector firmly against your thigh. This will release a spring-activated mechanism that injects a dose of epinephrine. Hold the auto-injector in place for a few seconds after activation. *The EpiPen should only be used on the fleshy outer portion of the thigh. You should not inject into a vein or the buttocks.*

4. Remove the auto-injector from your thigh and carefully reinsert the fired unit (without replacing the activation cap), needle first, into the amber carrying tube. Recap the amber tube.

5. Get to the emergency room immediately, and take the used EpiPen with you for proper disposal. (If you're alone, call 911. You should not drive if you're having an anaphylactic reaction.) Taking the EpiPen with you also ensures that the doctor knows you have had a shot of epinephrine and what amount you received.

Although you may not feel the medication being injected, it is released automatically when you activate the unit by pressing the auto-injector against your thigh. If you can see the needle when you remove the EpiPen from your thigh, the medication has been released. Don't worry if you notice a small amount of medication remaining in the EpiPen; it does not affect delivery of your dose. Each EpiPen delivers a single dose of epinephrine and cannot be used again.

No matter how well the EpiPen seems to have worked to ease symptoms, anyone who has had an anaphylactic reaction to nuts or peanuts should go to the emergency room. At least a third of patients who have had an anaphylactic reaction can have a second wave of symptoms several hours after the first attack. These second, or "late," reactions can sometimes be dangerous.

At the hospital, the patient may be given oxygen and intravenous fluids to treat low blood pressure. Experts usually recommend keeping an anaphylactic patient under observation at the hospital for six to twenty-four hours.

How Many Injections?

Epinephrine dosage is based on body weight. The EpiPen (0.3 mg) is prescribed for patients who weigh sixty-six pounds or more; the EpiPen Jr. (0.15 mg) is prescribed for individuals between thirty-three and sixty-six pounds.

Both strengths deliver a single dose, but since a single dose of epinephrine only lasts about twenty minutes, one dose may not be enough to completely reverse the effects of an anaphylactic reaction. A second dose also may be needed if it takes longer than twenty minutes to get to a hospital during a reaction and symptoms aren't subsiding.

Although occasionally in severe cases of anaphylaxis a patient may need more than one epinephrine injection, one injection is almost always enough to save a life. Too many injections of epinephrine can be dangerous. Your doctor will discuss with you your own limit; some patients can handle more or less epinephrine than the next patient. Your doctor will recommend either one or two injection kits for your particular situation.

Side Effects

Although epinephrine is an effective treatment for anaphylaxis, it's not without its own side effects. In order to understand these side effects, you'll need to understand the normal role that epinephrine (also known as adrenaline) plays within your body.

Epinephrine is a quick-acting hormone produced by two glands, one above each of your kidneys. In a crisis situation, epinephrine triggers the so-called "fight or flight" response, helping to prepare your body to take action by boosting your heart rate, widening your lungs' air passages, and constricting your blood vessels. A natural burst of epinephrine will make your heart pound, your hands shake, and your breath come in quick gasps.

When injected, epinephrine can offset all of the unpleasant effects of anaphylaxis. However, you inject epinephrine in higher amounts than your body would normally produce on its own, so you'll experience more side effects. Normal, expected side effects to epinephrine include trembling, heart palpitations, and a feeling of tension or anxiousness (although many people don't notice these symptoms). These effects soon wear off. However, at even larger doses, injected epinephrine may cause an extremely unpleasant feeling and may be dangerous to the heart.

These side effects are normally not serious if you use the right dose in the right way. But for some people who have other medical conditions, there are special risks that a doctor will need to consider before prescribing epinephrine. These special risks (which are quite rare in children) include high blood pressure, an abnormal heart rhythm, narrowing of the coronary arteries, or currently taking antidepressants. If you have any of these conditions, you should make sure the doctor knows before he or she prescribes epinephrine.

Care of Your EpiPen

The best way to protect your EpiPen is to keep it in its plastic tube, protected from direct sunlight, too much heat, and extreme cold. No epinephrine injection device must be allowed to freeze; it should be replaced if this happens accidentally. Light and heat can cause epinephrine to degrade, turning it brown and shortening its usable life. All medicines eventually deteriorate over time, and epinephrine can become less effective if it's outdated. You should always have a replacement on hand before the expiration date on the package passes.

The easiest way to make sure you do not forget to replace your EpiPen is to enroll in the EpiPen Expiration Reminder Program offered by the manufacturer. An enrollment form is included in each package, or you can enroll online at www.deyinc.com. This program will notify you one month before the expiration date so that you can get a prescription for a new EpiPen. The registration card also offers free educational information from patient support groups such as the Food Allergy and Anaphylaxis Network (FAAN) and MedicAlert.

Check your EpiPen periodically through its viewing window to make sure the solution is clear and colorless. Epinephrine that has turned yellow or brown is getting too old, although a color change does not always occur once the expiration date has passed.

In the Next Chapter

Knowing how to treat severe allergic reactions is extremely important. In the next chapter, we'll discuss how to manage your home so as to prevent as many reactions as possible.

5

Avoiding Exposure to Nuts and Peanuts

No matter how careful you are, it's almost inevitable that one day an allergic member of your family will eat a nut or peanut. Even in families who are extremely vigilant, there is an accidental exposure about once every two years.

The real challenge is to find the right balance between living in a safe environment, where the risk of exposure to nuts is minimized, and maintaining as few restrictions as possible. The way you manage the risk at your house may vary from one person to the next, depending on the allergic person's age, lifestyle, and the potential severity of his or her reactions. Still, it's comforting to know that while the risks of exposure to nuts can't be completely eliminated, they can be reduced by making careful choices at home.

You can minimize the exposure to nuts or peanuts by following this ten-step plan to keep your family member as safe as possible.

Step One: Avoid These Nuts and Peanuts

Avoidance is the main key in managing a peanut allergy, because the only way to prevent a nut or peanut allergic attack is to avoid all nuts or peanuts and their products. This means not eating or coming in contact with anything that has even minute traces of nuts or peanuts, including cooking and serving utensils and containers. It's important to remember that roasting or heating nuts does not make them safe to eat, nor does simply removing nuts from a dish.

The following tree nuts or peanuts are all capable of triggering an allergic response in sensitive individuals. Some people will be allergic to only one of these types of nuts, while many others will cross-react to more than one type.

- Almonds
- Almond extract
- Brazil nuts
- Cashews
- Chestnuts
- Filberts
- Hazelnuts

- Gianduja (a creamy mixture of chocolate and chopped toasted nuts found in premium or imported chocolate)
- Hickory nuts
- Macadamia nuts
- Marzipan
- Mashuga nuts (a type of Asian pecan)
- Nougat
- Nut butters (such as cashew or almond butter; many are made on machines used to process peanut butter)
- Nut meal
- Nut oil
- Nut paste (such as almond paste)
- Pecans
- Peanut butter
- Peanuts
- Pine nuts (also called pignolias, Indian nuts, or piñon nuts)
- Pistachios
- Walnuts

Step Two: Avoid Foods with Hidden Nuts

It's important to avoid obvious sources of nut or peanut proteins if you or a family member are allergic

Safe "Nuts"

Coconuts, nutmeg, and water chestnuts are all generally considered to be safe for people with a nut or peanut allergy, despite the fact that they have the word "nut" in their name.

A coconut is the seed of a drupaceous fruit, and is not typically restricted in the diet of an individual allergic to tree nuts. However, some people have reacted to coconut, so you should talk to a doctor before serving coconut.

Nutmeg is obtained from the seeds of the tropical tree species *Myristica fragrans* (the outer coating of the seed is ground to make mace). These ingredients should be safe for a person who is allergic to tree nuts.

The water chestnut is not a nut, but an edible portion of a plant root known as a *crom*. It's safe for someone who is allergic to tree nuts.

to nuts or peanuts. Foods that contain nuts, peanuts, or products made from nuts or peanuts may be labeled using words such as "nut or peanut extracts," "groundnuts," "mixed nuts," or "natural flavoring."

Be especially aware of packaged and processed foods, which may contain hidden nuts or peanuts.

A Word About Chocolate

I advise peanut-allergic patients to avoid chocolate candy unless they're absolutely certain there's no risk of cross-contamination during manufacturing. Many candy companies are aware of nut and peanut allergy issues and some make sure they manufacture nut-containing candy separately, so that people with nut allergies can still enjoy their products. To be sure a candy is nut- or peanut-free, log on to the manufacturer's website or call the toll-free number listed on the package. Most companies have customer service representatives who can answer these allergy questions accurately. When you call, be sure to tell the person you have a life-threatening allergy.

Processed foods to avoid because they may contain concealed nuts or peanuts include:

- Artificial nuts such as NuNuts (they could be peanuts that have been deflavored and reflavored with a nut flavoring, such as pecan or walnut)
- Asian foods (such as satay or pad thai)
- Baking mixes

- Baked goods
- Barbecue sauce
- Bouillon
- Cakes and pastries with unknown ingredients (especially carrot cake, pumpkin cake or pie, and fruit and nut rolls)
- Candy
- Cereals (especially those with fruit)
- Chili
- Cookies
- Dips
- Egg rolls
- Extracts such as natural wintergreen extract (for anyone who is allergic to filberts or hazelnuts)
- Flavoring (natural and artificial flavoring may contain tree nuts)
- Frangipane (a custard flavored with almonds)
- Fried foods (especially in fast-food restaurants); they may be made with peanut oil or may contain hidden peanuts or nuts
- Gravy
- Health-food bars
- Ice cream
- Liqueur (amaretto and Frangelico)
- Mandelonas (peanuts soaked in almond flavoring)
- Marzipan (a paste made from ground almonds and sugar)

- Mortadella (a type of smoked sausage that may contain pistachios)
- Muesli
- Nougat
- Oils (nut or peanut): cold-pressed peanut oil is usually not tolerated
- Peanut butter
- Peanut flour
- Pesto (an Italian sauce made with pine nuts)
- Praline (a paste of sugar and varying types of nuts)
- Salads and salad dressings
- Spaghetti sauce
- Sunflower seeds (many brands are produced on equipment shared with peanuts)
- Worcestershire sauce (may contain walnuts)

Step Three: Watch Out for Nonfood Products

Unfortunately, nuts are also used in unusual ways in a wide range of products and can sometimes be found in products that might not usually be associated with nuts at all. Nuts or peanuts can be ingredients in medications, cosmetics, pet food, toys, and furniture. If you're in doubt, call the manufacturer to check.

You might be surprised to find nuts or peanuts (or crushed shells) in the following nonfood items:

Peanut Oils

The process of refining oil removes the protein that would normally trigger an allergic reaction. Peanut oil (also called "arachis oil") is often used as a component in vegetable oil, in processed foods, or as an emulsifier or lubricant in cosmetics. The oil is highly refined, and should pose no problem for allergy sufferers. However, oils that are cold-pressed to retain their flavor, expelled or extruded peanut oil (sometimes represented as "gourmet oil"), and oil that has been used to cook peanuts, do contain the allergenic protein and therefore should be avoided. To be safe, you may want to avoid all peanut oils.

- Ant traps
- Beanbags
- Bird food
- Cosmetics (especially moisturizers)
- Dog food and treats (and dog saliva!)
- Hacky Sacks
- Hamster food and bedding
- Kick sacks
- Livestock feed
- Lotions

- Medications
- Mousetraps
- Secondhand toys and furniture
- Sunscreens
- Toiletries

Step Four: Read Labels

Government agencies have been working toward improving food ingredient labeling so allergic consumers can more easily determine which foods they need to avoid, but at present the situation is still far from perfect. Not all manufacturers use the voluntary statement that a product "may contain nuts or peanuts." Allergy organizations are trying to prod manufacturers into using simple language on their

Watch Out for Arachis Oil

Always check with your pharmacist to make sure any drugs, medications, or cosmetics are nut-free. When you're reading cosmetics labels, remember that many lotions, toiletries, and sunscreens may contain "arachis oil"—another name for "peanut oil." Discuss with your doctor whether you should avoid using these products.

ingredient lists so that even young children can understand them. They're also trying to get manufacturers to list all allergens, even those in very small amounts in flavors, colors, or spices.

In 1994, the Nutrition Labeling and Education Act required a major overhaul of food labels to make healthy eating easier. However, while food manufacturers are required to list every ingredient in a product, *there are a few exceptions*. Flavors, colors, spices, and ingredients that appear in insignificant (or trace) amounts don't have to be listed on food labels; these

Decoding Synonyms for Nuts

As you read, you may also come across ingredient names that mean nuts or peanuts but that don't have the word "nut" anywhere in sight. Here are a few ingredients to watch out for and avoid:

- Lecithins or "food additive 322"
- Arachis (an alternative term for peanut)
- Hydrolyzed vegetable protein (this may be found in some cereals)
- Ingredients that are "emulsified"
- Food labels using the word "satay" (this usually means a food or sauce has been thickened with peanuts)

could include nuts or peanuts and trigger an allergic reaction.

Always read all labels carefully, and teach others—including teachers and people who prepare food for you—to do the same. Once you get into the practice of reading food labels, you'll soon become familiar with technical or scientific names for foods. You should read labels of everything you eat—including other food in the house that others eat—because nuts and peanuts show up in the most amazing places!

If the food doesn't come with a label—such as certain baked goods, desserts, or other products from a bakery—and you don't know the ingredients, it's usually best to avoid it.

Step Five: Guard Against Cross-Contamination

At home, be on the watch for cross-contamination with knives or toasters. Make sure the knife used for making peanut butter sandwiches is not used to butter your bread and that nut breads are not toasted in the same toaster you use. Better yet, make sure your home is a nut-free zone. When it comes to food allergies, it is difficult to be careful enough. The same knife used to cut a peanut butter sandwich and a cheese sandwich can leave enough residue on the cheese sandwich to cause a serious allergic reaction. In fact, a Canadian girl died from this minimal amount of peanut exposure back in the mid-1990s. And remember—cross-contamination can also happen if someone with peanut residue on his or her hands touches someone with a nut allergy.

Industrial cross-contamination is a more serious issue. It's possible that a food that doesn't contain nut or peanut ingredients has been cross-contaminated if it's produced in a factory that also processes nuts or peanuts. This means that a factory may use the same equipment to process nuts as it does for products that don't contain nuts, and tiny amounts of nuts could be transferred to other foods. You may have seen warnings on some food labels that a food may contain trace amounts of nuts or peanuts, but these warnings are entirely up to the manufacturer. Fortunately, as awareness surrounding allergies grows, companies are taking steps to protect consumers.

Even if a particular variety of cookie does not contain any nuts, if it is produced using the same facilities as a walnut-topped cookie, for example, there is a chance that cross-contamination could take place in spite of vigorous industrial cleaning methods. This means that if a manufacturer makes several products with nuts, you probably don't want to purchase the one product they make without nuts.

Step Six: Don't Keep the Allergy Secret

For children with severe nut allergies, a peanut butter sandwich is every bit as dangerous as a loaded gun. Yet there exists an overwhelming lack of support for families who have children struggling with severe peanut and tree nut allergies.

One of the most important ways to minimize the risk of exposure to nuts or peanuts is by telling everyone about the family member's allergy. The more people who know about the problem, the less likely it is that an unsuitable food will be offered. Small children are amazingly good about avoiding nuts if they are allergic to them, and their parents don't make many mistakes. The main danger to children appears to come from mistakes made by adults other than their parents.

If it's your child who is allergic to peanuts or nuts, be sure that everyone who feeds and cares for the child knows about the allergy and what to do in case of an attack. This means the babysitter, teacher, school nurse, school cafeteria, and even friends need to be aware of the potential danger involved (for more information on talking to your child's school about nut allergy, see Chapter 8). Encourage people not to feed your child. Make your own snacks and treats to take to parties, play dates, sleepovers, school functions, and other outings.

Step Seven: Be Prepared

Unfortunately, it is virtually impossible to guarantee that a nut allergy patient will never come across the tiniest trace of nuts, no matter how careful the person might be. For this reason, it's vitally important that all patients who are allergic to peanuts or nuts set up an action plan to deal quickly with an accidental ingestion of nuts or peanuts.

When you're first diagnosed, your doctor will determine whether you should carry an EpiPen and use it in an emergency to counter a reaction. If your doctor prescribes an EpiPen, you should keep the device accessible at all times—not in the glove compartment of your car or your desk drawer at the office, but with you. Seconds count during anaphylaxis.

Anyone who has ever suffered a severe allergic reaction to nuts should always carry a minimum of two EpiPens at all times, since immediate treatment is vital should a severe allergic reaction occur.

Children who are allergic to nuts or peanuts are usually given several EpiPens for home and school. People who spend time around anyone who is allergic to nuts or peanuts—for example, the allergic person's spouse, coworkers, school teachers, or day care workers—should also know how to use an EpiPen.

Step Eight: Get a MedicAlert Bracelet

It's a good idea for anyone with a nut or peanut allergy to wear medical identification (such as a MedicAlert bracelet or necklace) describing the allergy and the person's susceptibility to anaphylaxis. This can ensure prompt, proper treatment during an emergency; in fact, a MedicAlert tag is the first thing emergency medical personnel look for when they respond to a call.

The MedicAlert organization provides members with an easily recognizable emblem available as a bracelet or necklace, engraved with the specific allergy and an 800 number accessible from anywhere in the world. Any doctor can call the number for more information about the patient's medical condition (available in more than 100 languages). If a call comes through, the MedicAlert staff also tries to reach the patient's family to let them know about the emergency.

It's especially important for children in late preschool to early elementary school to wear a Medic-Alert ID, since these youngsters are at an age when they are more likely to be occasionally on their own, yet not really old enough to communicate with others if they begin to experience an anaphylactic reaction. (You'll need to be vigilant, however, about the safety of such a child wearing a necklace around playground equipment; a bracelet may be a safer choice for this age group.) Very young children may not need such an ID because it would be quite unlikely for them to be left alone without being in the care of someone who knew their medical history. Older children may only need emergency ID if there is a risk of an abrupt allergic reaction.

If you're the one with the severe nut or peanut allergy and you're at risk for developing an anaphylactic reaction—so that you would not be able to administer an EpiPen or communicate with anyone else about your problem—a MedicAlert ID makes sense for you, too.

MedicAlert bracelets are available from the Medic-Alert Foundation, 2323 Colorado Avenue, Turlock, California 95382, (888) 633-4298, or at the website: www.medicalert.org. Membership is $35 for the first year, with an annual renewal fee of $20.

Step Nine: Educate Your Allergic Child

Having a nut- or peanut-allergic child is a sobering responsibility. Many parents of severely allergic children live with an incredible amount of stress when their child is away from home, knowing that an allergic reaction might occur. Some children are embarrassed, or cry, because they are different—not "like everybody else." Unfortunately, any child who is perceived as "different" may become the target of harassment by other children. Any instance in which a bullying child is physically threatening—especially by taunting the child with a nut or peanut product—must be immediately dealt with by intervening with the child's principal.

Other children worry about what will happen if they have a reaction so suddenly they can't tell an adult. Sometimes, these fears can spiral out of control, developing into a full-blown phobia about eating. Fortunately, most of these anxieties can be dealt with by calmly addressing the concerns and helping your child develop the self-confidence to handle any situation.

If you're the parent of a nut-allergic child, you must educate your children early and often, not only about the allergy itself but also about what reaction they'll have if they eat the offending food. Empower your children to take responsibility for their allergy—children as young as two can begin to learn that they have an allergy. Explain why it's important to wear a MedicAlert bracelet (if your child has one) and why EpiPens must always be carried. Try to explain these issues calmly and matter-of-factly, assuring your worried child that you will keep him safe.

Be sure your child understands that he must not only ask about the presence of nuts, but also explain that he has a severe, life-threatening allergy. Too many people don't take the nut allergy situation seriously enough. Read books to your child to explain nut and peanut allergies. Buy books for your child's classroom, school, and local library to explain these allergies.

The hard part of parenting an allergic child is that outside the home, many other parents and children just don't understand the issues, nor do they understand the risks of cross-contamination. Most don't realize that even a tiny crumb of a nut or peanut can trigger a severe reaction. All too often, you'll find that others may dismiss your concerns as being "overpro-tective" ("Surely just one cookie won't hurt.").

Some parents believe that having a child be responsible for her own allergy means she won't take food from anyone, or touch food outside the home. Others believe their child is responsible enough to always ask, "Are there nuts in this?" before eating. Eventually your child will be able to carry her own EpiPen, and you'll be able to count on her ability to stay away from nuts or peanuts on her own.

At the same time, it's important not to overprotect your child. Work together with your spouse, and try not to make non-allergic siblings feel left out or unnec-essarily restricted by the allergy.

Step Ten: Cleanup Tips for Removing Nut Residue

Because peanut or nut residue on countertops, cutlery, or plates may induce a reaction in a severely allergic individual, it's important to prevent accidental contact by thoroughly washing any dishes, worktops, or uten-sils that have been in contact with nuts or peanuts. Unfortunately, no scientific studies have been done to evaluate cleaning practices or methods in the removal of food proteins, but warm soapy water appears to be an excellent way of safely cleaning tables, utensils, and so on. Removing the food from the surface should be

Books About Nut Allergies

The following books are appropriate for children between the ages of four and eight:

- *Allie the Allergic Elephant: A Children's Story of Peanut Allergies* by Nicole Smith (Jungle Communications, 2002)
- *No Nuts for Me* by Aaron Zevy and Susan Tebbutt (Tumbleweed Press, 1996)
- *The Peanut Butter Jam* by Elizabeth Sussman Nassau and Margot J. Ott (Health Press, 2001)

the main goal, and any wet cleaner together with vigorous wiping should be enough. Waterless cleaners or instant hand sanitizers that do not include a wet-wash/wipe step would not be adequate.

The most important thing is to use a fresh cloth or paper towels when cleaning the allergic person's area, to avoid cross-contamination from a sponge or cloth that was used to clean allergen-containing tabletops. Hand washing after food handling should be encouraged in day care and preschool settings, as well as in lower schools. Once again, soap and warm water should be sufficient.

Managing Nut and Peanut Allergies

A diagnosis of a nut or peanut allergy can have a dramatic impact on your life. The first task you must deal with is to make sure that your home is a safe haven. Once you've passed this hurdle, a continuing range of new challenges will present themselves, especially if you have nut-allergic children: how to handle birthday parties, sleepovers, holiday celebrations, day care and preschool, and college life.

All of these experiences can cause potential problems and must be prepared for with a positive outlook; this is important because the allergic child will adopt and reflect the attitude of the parents. Constant uncontrolled anxiety will affect both parents and child and can have a negative impact on family relationships. Instead, parents should try to make the child feel as normal and natural as possible while providing maximum protection.

Children's Parties

Children's parties are a common childhood experience, but for the allergic child (and her parents) they can pose particular problems. On these festive occasions, there is likely to be at least some unsuitable foods readily offered to the children.

If the kind hostess offers to make the party "nut-free"—not that easy given typical party foods that include cakes, cookies, ice cream, and chocolate—it's important to make sure she understands what "nut-free" really means. Most parents without an allergic child assume "nut-free" simply means no visible nuts; they aren't accustomed to scrutinizing labels to find hidden ingredients. They don't understand that a plain chocolate bar could still be cross-contaminated with nuts during the manufacturing process, or that the bakery birthday cake could contain hidden ground nuts.

Discussing all these issues before the party can help avoid embarrassment—or a serious allergic reaction. Probably it would be more realistic for you to provide a separate box of safe food from your home for the allergic child. And if you do provide your own food, it's also a good idea to ask the party hostess to avoid extremely high-risk foods, such as peanut butter, that might pose a threat simply by their presence at the party table. This is especially important at parties with very small children, who tend to wander around with food coating their fingers or dropping food on the floor.

Most children's parties these days include a "party bag" of treats for each child to take home. The party host might appreciate it if you could provide a separate "party bag" of safe snacks and sweets to give the child when it's time to go home.

Feeding an allergic child before the party lessens the risk of nibbling during the festivities, but most allergic children won't object to eating different food, especially if the child knows that the food from home is safe. You need to remember that it's important for nut-allergic children to accept the idea that they won't always be able to eat the same foods as their friends.

If your child requires an EpiPen to treat severe reactions, you'll need to leave it at the party and make sure there is someone trained to handle that responsibility—if there isn't, you'll need to stay. If the host is comfortable with the idea and well-trained in handling nut allergies, you'll need to make sure to leave Benadryl on hand as well (to treat hives), and to make sure the host knows that if your child has had an allergic reaction, he must be taken to the emergency room even if an EpiPen is used. Some hosts will be more willing than others to accept the responsibility of a nut-allergic child at a birthday party. In any case, most parents of young allergic children prefer to stay and help with the party to monitor the peanut situation and to be available if a problem develops.

Adopting House Rules

If someone in your home has a nut allergy, over the years you'll devise your own ways of dealing with problems. Some people choose to make their home a completely nut-free zone, with absolutely no nuts, nut-containing products, or nut-contaminated products allowed. Other families may decide that nuts and nut products are allowed, but that they must be kept completely separate from other food in the house. What's most important is that everyone in the home agrees on the rules and works together to make sure the rules are upheld.

Guests and visitors to a totally nut-free home also need to understand the rules, so they know what foods not to bring into the house (including chocolates or baked goods). This can be more difficult than it sounds, especially with close relatives, who may not understand the seriousness of nut allergies and assume you are being overly fussy or hypervigilant. Clear explanations of why the rules are enforced, with specific and blunt information about the consequences if these rules are broken, usually help. Visitors need to understand that the no-nut rule is literally a matter of life and death.

Shopping with Nut Allergies

Most people find food shopping an endless chore, but for someone with a nut or peanut allergy, it can be a nightmare. Food labels need to be checked to make sure there are no nuts or nut derivatives at every shopping visit, since the ingredients could have changed since the food was purchased the last time. All food ingredient labels need to be checked.

Visiting Friends in Their Home

It's always a challenge when a family that has a nut-allergic individual gets invited to eat at the home of friends or family. With luck, your hosts will understand the problems this can create, but you'll need to help guide them as to what exactly a "nut-free" diet means. It's hard enough for the nut-allergic individual to maintain a safe, nut-free diet; you can't expect others to be able to manage this without some help. The easiest way to handle the problem of safe dining at others' houses is to plan a meal or snack with the host so that you can avoid the embarrassment of having to refuse food that your friends have prepared.

If your allergic child is invited to a young friend's house, it's often easiest to send the child with safe food from home. Otherwise, parents must check with the guest family that all food, snacks, and treats are safe. If the child is staying overnight with a friend and normally carries rescue medication, the host will need to be carefully instructed on how and when to administer the medication in the unlikely event that it is needed. The host must also understand that the medication must be brought along on any trips from the house, no matter how short. Some families find it helpful to send along a laminated card with instructions on handling an allergic reaction:

In Case of Allergic Reaction

1. For hives: give ＿＿＿＿＿ tablets of Benadryl.
2. For breathing trouble: administer an EpiPen immediately. Then get to an emergency room as quickly as possible.

At the Holidays

The holidays come with many tempting dishes and treats. It's very important, this time of year, to ask questions and be extra careful to avoid hidden or surprise ingredients.

To minimize food allergy risks over the holidays, stress to family and friends how serious nut and peanut allergies can be—and emphasize that allergic reactions can be fatal. Alert holiday party hosts about the nut or peanut allergy and clarify all ingredients used to prepare foods. Many people with nut allergies have learned to eat before attending special events in case the foods that are served contain allergens.

Of all the holidays, Halloween can be a particularly stressful time for the nut-allergic child, who wants to gather and eat treats just like his friends. Many parents have found that their child is satisfied with fun toys or other non-food items for Halloween. Some parents feel comfortable telling their allergic child that hard candies or lollipops are okay—as long as the child waits until he or she gets home before eating anything.

Before trick-or-treat night, you may want to drop off with the neighbors some safe treats or little toys such as stickers, little plastic toys, or yo-yos. You can tell your neighbors what the child will be wearing and accompany him to the door to make sure the neighbors remember what treats to provide.

New Legislation

The U.S. Senate has recently passed the Food Allergen Labeling and Consumer Protection Act (FAL-CPA), which requires food processors to identify all major allergens contained in a food item. If also passed by the House of Representatives, it will take effect on January 1, 2006.

This groundbreaking legislation is the result of years of hard work by federal legislators, the food industry, the U.S. Food and Drug Administration (FDA), and other consumer advocacy groups. The bill requires food allergen statements to be clear, consistent, and reliable. FALCPA defines the term "major food allergen" as including tree nuts and peanuts as well as milk, eggs, fish, crustaceans, shell-fish, wheat, and soybeans. If passed, food manufactured on or after January 1, 2006, would have to declare major food allergens in its ingredient list or by using the word "contains," followed by the name of the major food allergen (peanut or tree nut), or a parenthetical statement in the list of ingredients, such as "tree nut (walnut)." Flavorings, colorings, and incidental additives that contain a major food allergen must be declared. Further, the bill asks the Secretary of Health and Human Services to submit a report to Congress on cross-contact during food manufacturing and processing and ways to avoid it; the use of advisory labeling ("may contain") by the food industry; consumer opinion on advisory labeling; and how the industry is doing with respect to cross-contact and labeling. The law also requires the Department of Health and Human Services to inspect facilities where food is manufactured, processed, packed, or held; collect and publish data on the prevalence, incidence, and treatment of food allergy; convene an expert panel to review current research on food allergy; consider creating guidelines for preparing allergen-free foods in restaurants, grocery store delis and bakeries, and school cafeterias; and help state and local emergency medical services treat allergic reactions.

In the Next Chapter

Avoiding exposure to nuts and peanuts is only the beginning of the battle. Eating out in restaurants poses a big risk for anyone allergic to nuts or peanuts. In the next chapter, we'll discuss how to prevent problems when dining out.

6

Eat, Drink, and Be Wary: Avoiding Nuts and Peanuts in Restaurants

ane K., 42, was celebrating her birthday with friends at a local restaurant. Her waiter assured her several times that her meal was completely nut-free, and explained that the restaurant had listings of all ingredients of the dishes posted in the kitchen. But seconds after tasting her pasta sauce, Jane felt her mouth start to tingle, and then her throat begin to swell shut. Staffers quickly called a cab and rushed her to a nearby hospital, where she was treated for an anaphylactic reaction to the dish—which had contained nuts. The harried waiter had quickly checked the list of ingredients, but hadn't noticed that nuts were listed.

Whether you're eating at a café, a fast-food outlet, or a fancy four-star restaurant, the lack of total control over food preparation can be a challenge if you're allergic to nuts or peanuts. That's why it shouldn't come as a surprise that most allergic reactions to nuts happen when people are eating in restaurants. This is because most nut-allergic people are so sensitive to nut allergens that if peanuts or nuts are used anywhere in a restaurant, accidents are quite likely to occur despite everyone's best efforts.

Beware of These Restaurants

You *can* eat out in restaurants if you have a nut or peanut allergy, but you have to be vigilant. Some types of restaurants are so likely to pose high risks for nut or peanut allergy sufferers that the most realistic approach is simply to avoid them. These include restaurants specializing in African, Chinese, Indonesian, Mexican, Thai, and Vietnamese dishes, which often contain peanuts or peanut oil, and which may be prepared in a kitchen where the foods come into contact with nuts or peanuts.

Bakeries and ice cream shops often keep peanuts on hand, or produce food on equipment that's also used to process peanuts. In some Asian restaurants, crushed nuts might be added to your meal by a busy chef who may not have understood why you ordered a nut-free dish. Nut allergy is rare in Asian countries, so Asian restaurateurs may not realize the seriousness of the problem.

If you eat in these restaurants, you're liable to eat nuts sooner or later, despite your best intentions and those of the staff. In Asian restaurants, foods often contain many ingredients and nuts may be harder to spot individually. Furthermore, spicy food may mask the immediate tingling sensations in the mouth often triggered by nut allergies. Finally, language problems may make it harder to ensure that you and the staff understand each other.

If you have a nut allergy, you're also at fairly high risk if you eat at a bakery or café, since nuts are often used as an ingredient for cakes and pastries and the likelihood of cross-contamination is high in these kind of open environments. That's why I recommend that people with nut or peanut allergies should avoid these types of restaurants.

Even if you've visited a particular restaurant or fast-food chain safely in the past, you'll need to check ingredients each time you visit, since recipes can often change. This is also why you should never eat in a restaurant without your EpiPen. (It's also a good idea to eat with at least one person who knows your problem and knows how to use the EpiPen.)

Remember that nuts may lurk not just in a particular dish. Cooking in peanut oil may leave traces of nut protein in the food being cooked. Any oil that has previously been used to cook products containing nuts may contain traces of nut proteins. Salad dressing may be made from peanut oil. And many dishes (such as chili) may contain hidden nuts or peanuts.

When You Arrive

When you walk in the door, don't be shy—tell all the employees you meet (waitstaff, hosts, sommelier, and chef) that someone at your table has a nut allergy. Servers need to understand that your request to avoid nuts is not fussy behavior, but based on the real risk that exposure to nuts or peanuts could cause a potentially fatal reaction. Servers need to know about the allergy, about the risks posed by contamination, and about the potential severity of the reaction if nut products are served. Many food servers don't realize that being asked if something "has nuts in it" refers to nuts in *all* forms, including peanut butter or walnut oil. In fact, it is these "hidden nuts" that cause the most problems for allergic diners.

Don't mince words. State the extreme risk clearly if death is a risk at all, even a tiny risk: "I am dangerously allergic to nuts, and if I eat anything with even the tiniest trace of nut I might die." You can't get much clearer than that.

If the manager, the chef, or the owner of a restaurant is uncomfortable about your request for peanut- or nut-free food preparation, leave.

After You Order

Even if you tell restaurant staff the problem, they are often extremely busy and may not have your unusual needs at the forefront of their minds every moment while handling your food. Quite often a busy waitperson may say things are nut-free without actually checking. In the end, you can't place the entire burden for your safety on restaurant staff.

If you're buying fried foods such as fish and chips or chicken, always remember to ask what kind of oil the food is fried in. Waiters don't normally see food being prepared and may not know what type of oil is used, so speak to the chef if possible.

If your ice cream is served covered with nuts, it's a good idea to keep the offending dish at your table to make sure you get a new, uncontaminated serving. In some busy restaurants, unaware waiters simply scrape off the nuts and cover the ice cream with more whipped cream.

More and more restaurants are becoming aware of the existence of severe allergies. Some fast-food chains, for example, offer pamphlets listing the ingredients of all the entrees; some chains even have a specific nut policy. For example, many Dairy Queens and Mrs. Field's Cookies restaurants post signs indicating that all of their products may have been exposed to nuts, because nuts are used in so many of their foods that cross-contamination is likely. Chick-fil-A generally uses peanut oil for all of their cooking.

In general, however, most restaurants and hotels are probably not that safe unless they have very special arrangements in place. Without such a precaution, there is always the possibility of cross-contamination of foods. Even if you explain yourself properly to the staff and don't end up eating something which has nuts put in intentionally, all it takes is for someone to move a utensil from one pot to another to transfer a trace of nuts to the food you're going to eat.

Even while restaurant staffers are increasingly aware of the problem and are usually doing their best, many families who deal with nut allergies believe eating out in restaurants is just not worth the risk.

Rules for a Sensitive Restaurateur

Hosts, waitstaff, and chefs all should listen carefully and sympathetically to any customer who asks about ingredients, and take their questions seriously. Restaurant staffers should always tell the truth about what's in a dish—if you don't know, or aren't sure, you should never guess. There should always be at least one staff member on duty who has access to accurate ingredient information, so that staff with questions about any dish on the menu can go to that person for help. Ideally, lists should be posted in the kitchen so waitstaff can check if there is any question.

Customers with allergies should be encouraged to question staff. Some restaurants have found it helpful to post the following prominent statement on the menu: "Some of our dishes contain nuts. If you are allergic to nuts, please ask the waiter to suggest a nut-free meal."

Restaurant managers can minimize risks by avoiding situations where cross-contamination can occur. Suppliers should provide accurate written details about all ingredients, including any planned changes. Chefs should try to avoid using chopped nuts as a garnish, unless this is an essential part of the recipe.

If a dish contains nuts, it should be reflected in the name: for example, "walnut and apple salad." If possible, certain preparation areas should be designated as "nut-free."

Restaurant managers should train staffers about allergies, and make sure all new staff members (including part-time employees) are aware of serious allergies and know how to handle customer questions.

If a waiter has any doubt about whether a food is free of nuts, he or she should admit this to the customer and make an effort to find out. If, on examining a meal, a customer realizes it contains nuts and asks a waitperson to replace it, it is not enough simply to pick the nuts from the plate and return the plate to the customer. The tiny traces that remain may be enough to cause a severe allergic reaction. If there is a cake covered in nuts on the dessert tray, waitstaff should make sure no nuts could possibly be transferred to adjacent desserts.

In an Emergency

Staff trained in first aid should make a point of learning how to recognize allergic symptoms and what to do if someone experiences anaphylaxis. If an allergic diner begins to have a severe allergic reaction to nuts or peanuts in the restaurant, someone should immediately dial 911 and provide the following information:

1. "This is an emergency. A customer has collapsed and is suffering from anaphylaxis."
2. Give the address clearly so the ambulance will know exactly where to come.
3. Send someone to the restaurant entrance to direct the ambulance crew to the patient.
4. Ask other customers if there is a doctor in the restaurant.

In the Next Chapter

Learning how to cope with nut and peanut allergies while dining out is important. In the next chapter, we'll take it a step further and discuss strategies for safe travel.

7

Avoiding Nuts When on the Go

No matter how safe you may have made your home, job, or school, once you decide to travel out into the world there are new challenges to consider. The good news is that there are now more options than ever for travelers with peanut or nut allergies. It may help to keep in mind that lots of nut-sensitive people have traveled safely all around the world without a problem—and with a little preparation, you can too.

Your doctor can help you assess the risks involved in your specific case. By taking the precautions that we'll discuss in this chapter, you'll significantly reduce the risk of severe allergic reaction on your travels.

Air Travel

Airlines today are far more aware of the dangers that nuts and peanuts can pose to some of their passengers than ever before. Domestic carriers who don't serve peanut snacks include United, U.S. Air, American, Northwest, Jet Blue, Spirit, and Delta. Other airlines continue to serve some tree nut mixtures in first class, or as part of a snack mix in coach.

International carriers who don't serve peanut snacks include Aer Lingus, British Airways, Air Canada, and El Al. The use of peanuts is forbidden in any British Airways food preparations, including the use of derivatives such as peanut oil. (The one exception is that a limited amount of satay is allowed on selected Far Eastern routes in first class only, and always providing that the contents of the meal are clearly printed on the menu.) The service of peanuts as a cocktail accompaniment is allowed in first class, in "Club World" (the British Airways version of "business class"), and in premium (exclusive) airport lounges.

American Airlines serves pretzels in the main or coach cabins on most flights. Although they still serve peanuts on some flights and say they will continue to do so, American will remove the peanuts from snacks and meals served in the main or coach cabin on a particular flight if passengers do two things:

- Call (800) 433-7300 to make a reservation and advise the representative of the peanut allergy. Once your reservation has been completed, ask to be transferred to the Special Assistance Coordinator's Desk to request that peanuts be removed from the flight.
- Submit a medical verification stating the existence of a severe peanut allergy, signed by a medical doctor who is not a family member. This may be faxed to AA's Special Assistance Coordinator's Desk at (817) 967-4715.

Both of these requirements must be completed prior to seven days before the scheduled flight.

Northwest Airlines will also make special accommodations for customers with severe nut or peanut allergies. You will need to advise the reservations department of your special dietary requirements when you call to book the flight, so that the catering service can supply suitable meals and refrain from using peanuts in the in-flight meals and the packaged snacks given at boarding time. In addition, Ground Operations staff will make appropriate announcements on the flights concerned. Northwest Airlines was one of the first airlines to establish a direct radio linkup to the Director of Aeronautical Medicine at the Mayo Clinic, which can be accessed from anywhere in the world twenty-four hours a day.

Unfortunately, there are still some carriers who will not make accommodations for passengers with peanut allergy (including Continental, ATA, and America West).

While peanuts and nuts are not banned outright on all airplanes, in 1998 the U.S. Department of Transportation informed all large American airlines that they must set aside a "peanut-free zone" when requested to do so by passengers with medically documented peanut allergies. The minimum peanut-free zone is the row of seating with the allergic passenger plus the rows in front and behind.

However, remember that just because an airline does not serve peanut or nut snacks doesn't mean you're safe—the airline may include peanut ingredients in their meals, or other passengers may carry peanuts on the plane with them. This is why no airline can *guarantee* a peanut-free flight, although many do the best they can.

Reservation Tips

In order to be as safe as you can, here's what to do when contemplating airline travel with an allergic flier in your family.

- Try to book your trip so you are traveling early in the morning rather than late at night. On an evening flight, there is a higher chance that passengers may eat peanuts with an alcoholic drink.
- When booking reservations, always reconfirm the airline's peanut or nut snack policy, because airlines may change their policy without notice. Even if an airline normally serves peanuts or nuts on flights, many are willing to serve non-nut snacks such as pretzels to everyone on the flight (or at least in the guest's immediate vicinity) if a peanut-allergic passenger asks them to do so when making a reservation.
- Call the airline's customer service representative directly and tell him or her what you need. The airline's customer service representative or supervisor is more likely to know of any changes in policy.
- Ask for "no nuts." No matter which airline you choose, tell them when booking your flight that you're asking for a non-peanut or non-nut snack for *everyone* on your flight. If the reservation agent doesn't seem to understand what you're asking for, ask to speak to a supervisor or special service coordinator (titles vary by airline).

- When you call in your "no nuts" request, be sure to give plenty of notice. The more time you give an airline to prepare a nut-free flight, the more likely it is that they will be able to honor your request.
- Don't have someone else make your reservations (such as a travel agent) to book flights for you, and don't book your flights online. If you book through a third party, the agent may delay giving your special request to the airline.
- Ask for a written confirmation of your request and the airline's response (some will provide it and others won't, but it may help if you have to reschedule your flights en route).
- Obtain the name and telephone number of a supervisor or special service coordinator in case you have a problem en route.
- Have allergy documentation on hand from your doctor; some airlines insist on having documentation before providing a nut-free snack.

Carrying EpiPens on Board

Although new airline security regulations restrict a wide variety of items onboard, such as scissors and box openers, patients with nut or peanut allergies can still carry an EpiPen on commercial airlines, as long as they follow certain guidelines. The Transportation Security Administration (TSA) has ruled that you can bring syringes containing medication on board an airplane, provided that the syringe has a professionally printed label identifying the medication or the manufacturer's name. It's probably still a good idea to carry additional documentation such as a doctor's note (see page 104) and the prescription label from the pharmacy.

Preparing for the Trip

Once your airline reservations are made, your job's not over yet. There are still a number of important things to do before, during, and after your flight:

Before you go:
- Before you leave, discuss your travel plans in detail with your allergist, set up a plan to handle possible emergencies, and make sure you obtain a letter from the allergist confirming the nut or peanut allergy.
- Pack a container with your own safe food (in case you can't find acceptable food on the trip). Carry enough peanut- or nut-free food with you to last for your whole trip. As an extra precaution, the allergic traveler may simply want to avoid eating airline meals. Because

Sample Doctor's Letter for EpiPen

To Whom It May Concern:

_____ (patient's full name) suffers from a life-threatening allergy to tree nuts and/or peanuts. This allergy can cause a severe allergic reaction that must be treated immediately with an EpiPen, which is an auto-injector of epinephrine. EpiPen auto-injectors are prescribed by a licensed medical professional.

_____ (patient's name) must carry this lifesaving medication at all times, especially during travel away from home. In the event of an exposure to even a minute amount of allergen, a severe allergic reaction may occur. Every minute is critical in using this medication to treat the allergic reaction and to prevent a life-threatening reaction. Use of the EpiPen can be lifesaving. Please allow (patient's name) to have the EpiPen on board the airplane.

More information may be obtained from _____ (doctor's name) at _____ (phone number).

of the risk of flight delays or cancellations, bring enough food for at least two extra meals.

- Bring your own cutlery, because that will lessen the risk of contamination. Pack the cutlery at the top of your bag in case of security checks, but do not bring sharp knives. Standard kitchen cutlery (or plasticware) is fine.

- Pack your own medical kit in your carry-on luggage in case your checked luggage is delayed.

- Obtain a small wallet-sized laminated card before you leave that includes medical emergency steps to take in the event of a reaction. You also can get a card laminated with a list of all the hidden ingredients that you or your child need to watch for. This card can be given to the waitstaff or the chef to use as a guide when preparing food for the person with the allergy. (For cards in other languages, contact the appropriate embassy or consulate to find out how to get the information translated.)

- Be sure to take your physician's phone number with you.

At the airport:
- Arrive at the airport early and confirm your nut-free snack request at the gate, and again with the flight attendant when you get on the plane.

- If the gate agent tells you there is no record of the request, have the agent call the special service coordinator who helped with your reservation.
- If you are traveling with another person, give that person one of your EpiPens to carry. That way, if your bag gets lost, you'll still have a backup.
- When you are checking in, ask if the flight is full or empty; if it's not completely filled, ask for a seat away from other passengers.
- Try to board early so you can clean your seating area before others board the plane.

On the plane:
- As soon as you board the plane, notify the flight attendants of your nut allergy. They should be aware that you may need medical attention.
- As soon as you get to your seat, wipe down the seats, armrests, tray table, and window area with a disposable wipe. Inspect the floor and seat area and remove any peanut residue from previous flights.
- If a reaction occurs, follow your doctor's orders and notify the flight crew immediately. The crew can identify health professionals on board who can help, contact doctors on the ground, or allow the pilot to begin preparations to land the plane, if necessary.

If You Have a Problem

To resolve any problems you encountered during a flight, you can report the incident in writing to the airline chief executive officer and to the Aviation Consumer Protection Division (ACPD), which operates a complaint-handling system for consumers who experience air travel service problems. Consumers with concerns about airline safety or security should call the Federal Aviation Administration at (800) 255-1111. Consumers can call the ACPD with concerns at (202) 366-2220 (TTY 202-366-0511). The mailing address is ACPD, U.S. Department of Transportation, 400 Seventh Street SW, Washington, D.C. 20590. The e-mail address is: airconsumer@ost.dot.gov, and the ACPD website address is: http://aircon sumer.ost.dot.gov

All Aboard!

Train travel for the most part isn't exactly what it used to be; meals in the dining car on many trips mean a sandwich or plastic-wrapped meal from vendors on the train. Most families with nut-sensitive members bring their own safe foods.

Cruising Around

One of the biggest attractions on most cruises is the lavish meals offered just about twenty-four hours a day. While some ships cater to passengers with special diets, just about any ship will try to accommodate someone with allergic requirements. However, it's always a good idea to let the cruise line know before you sail that someone with a severe allergy and/or asthma will be traveling on board. While most cruise ships have extensive medical services available on board, it's a good idea to check to make sure your cruise line has what you might need.

Disney Cruise Lines has specifically trained their staff in understanding food allergies. Carnival Cruise Lines indicates that guests requiring special meals should make those requests at least two weeks before departure. The Cunard line requires thirty days' notice for special requests. In addition, it's a good idea to check with the waitstaff on any cruise ship to make sure they are aware of your special allergic needs.

At the Hotel

If you're planning to stay in a hotel or a bed-and-breakfast, ask in advance if there are nut or peanut allergy–proof rooms available. At a minimum, ask for a room with air conditioning and portable air filters.

Check with the reception staff upon arrival about the location of the nearest hospital. Ask if they have an in-house doctor and local phone numbers required in case of an emergency.

Traveling Abroad

If you're planning an overseas trip, you'll need to take extra precautions to make sure you'll be understood when eating in restaurants, to ascertain where medical care can be found, and to be sure you have proper health insurance coverage. Europeans have been aware of peanut and nut allergies since the early 1900s.

Canadians are particularly sensitive to the subject. Many restaurants throughout Canada participate in a program called "Allergy Aware," which offers diners information on ingredients in their menus. In order to participate in the program, the restaurant must provide a food allergy chart for at least three main menu items and complete ingredient information on at least three main menu items or three special meals. You can check for the special "Allergy Aware" symbol in Canadian restaurant windows.

Of course, any medications and EpiPens carried overseas should be left in their original containers and be clearly labeled. Travelers should check with the foreign embassy of the country they are visiting to make sure any required medications are not considered to be illegal narcotics. When traveling abroad, make sure to carry your physician's phone number at all times. Always remember to bring along a doctor's letter (see box on page 104) certifying the need to carry EpiPens and any other medications.

Bring extra "safe" food with you when traveling, just in case you experience any travel delays.

To help medical workers understand your problem if you have an allergic reaction, be sure to wear a medical alert bracelet (see Chapter 5) and complete the information page on the inside of your passport providing the name, address, and telephone number of someone to be contacted in an emergency.

Health Insurance Abroad

If you're going to be traveling abroad, don't forget to check whether your health insurance covers you when you're out of the country. Most health insurance companies, HMOs, PPOs, and Medicare do not offer such coverage. (If your company does offer this insurance, it probably won't include your evacuation back to the United States.)

Senior citizens may wish to contact the American Association of Retired Persons for information about foreign medical care coverage with Medicare supplement plans.

If your policy doesn't cover you when you're traveling abroad or doesn't cover repatriation services, you might consider buying an international travel medical insurance policy (see the Appendix for a list of international health insurance companies).

If your health insurance policy does provide coverage outside the United States, make sure to obtain copies of all bills and receipts (preferably in English) and carry both your insurance policy identity card (as proof of insurance) and a claim form with you.

Overseas physicians and hospitals may require payment in cash for services rendered and may accept a credit card. If an American citizen becomes seriously ill with a nut-related allergic reaction while abroad, a U.S. consular officer can help locate appropriate med-

Foreign Language Cards

DietaryCard.com offers an online service for people with all types of nut allergies who would like to purchase credit-card size cards with custom-made explanations of their dietary needs in Spanish, French, Italian, German, or English. The cards cost $7 each or $21 for all five. See the Resources section for contact information.

ical services and inform family or friends. If necessary, a consular officer can also help transfer money from the United States.

A listing of addresses and telephone numbers of U.S. embassies and consulates abroad is contained in *Key Officers of Foreign Service Posts*, which you can obtain through the Superintendent of Documents, U.S. Government Printing Office, Washington, D.C., 20402.

Foreign Terms

Communication is a big issue when it comes to international travel for people with severe nut or peanut allergies. You can buy special cards describing your allergic problem in different foreign languages (see page 111). It also makes sense to learn a few key phrases in the language of the country where you'll be visiting, using the following individual foreign phrases.

French   The French translation for "I am allergic to nuts" is "Je suis allergique aux noix," pronounced "jhuh sweez ah-lehr-jheek OH NWA." The French have several different terms for "nut," including:

- Pistache [pea-STASH] = pistachio
- Arachide [ah-rah-SHEED] = groundnut or peanut

- Cacahuète [KAK-a-wet] = peanut
- Noisette [nwa-SET] = hazelnut or nut
- Beurre de cacahuètes [BURR-duh-KAK-a-wet] = peanut butter
- Noix [nwa] = nut or walnut
- Amande [ah-MAHND] = almond
- Châtaigne [cha-TAHN-ya] = chestnut
- Noix de pecan or pacane [nwa-duh-pah-KAHN] = pecan

German Pecans are quite uncommon in Europe, so there is no word in German for them. But marzipan is a very common confection, which is made with ground almonds and sugar. (Cheaper versions often have other nuts in them as well, to stretch the almonds.)

In German, " I am allergic to nuts" would be: "Ich bin allergisch gegen Nüsse," pronounced "ish bin al-air-gish gai-ghen nuh-se."

- Nüss or Nüsse [nous] = nut
- Erdnüss [EHRD-nous] = peanut
- Walnüss [VAHL-nous] = walnut
- Haselnüss [HAH-zel-nous] = hazelnut
- Mandel [MAHN-dl] = almond
- Erdnüssöl [EHRD-nous-eul] = peanut oil
- Erdnüssbutter [EHRD-nous-buh-ter] = peanut butter

Spanish The following terms are used throughout Mexico and Latin America:

- Cacahuete [kaka-WAY-tay] = peanut
- Manteca de cacahuete [mahn-TAY-ka day kaka-WAY-tay] or manilla [mahn-EE-ya] = peanut butter
- Aceite de cacahuete [ah-SAY-tay day kaka-way-tay] = peanut oil
- Nuez [noo-ayz] = nut

However, in Spain natives also say "frutas secas" (as in dried fruits, but this refers to nuts), pronounced "FRUIT-ahs SAY-kas."

In Andalucia (south of Spain) the word "avellana," pronounced "ah-vay-AN-a," is commonly used to denote peanuts, even though it actually means "hazelnut."

Dutch Dutch names (same spelling in Flemish) for nuts are:

- Pindanoot [PIN-da-note] = peanut
- Pindakaas [PIN-dah-kaz] = peanut butter
- Aardnoot [ART-note], aardnoten
- Apenoot [AHP-note]

In the Next Chapter

Safe travel takes careful planning. In the next chapter, we'll see how such planning can also keep children safe at school.

8

Nut and Peanut Allergies at School

Schools may not be the haven of safety we like to think they are—at least for children with nut or peanut allergies. In a chilling study from Johns Hopkins University that studied thirteen children with life-threatening nut allergies who had died or almost died, scientists found that the six children who died had had an allergic reaction after eating nuts while at school. In each of the fatal cases, after eating nuts each child had immediately gone to the school nurse, who instructed the child to lie down and see if she or he felt better. Each of them did feel better, returned to class—and died.

Of course, fatal reactions to nut allergies are still rare, and it's important to remember that there are different levels of peanut allergies. Some children are so allergic to nuts or peanuts that even inhaling the nut dust will trigger an anaphylactic reaction. Other children react by getting hives after touching nuts or peanuts. Still others have a reaction only if they eat a product made from peanuts or nuts.

If your child has a nut or peanut allergy, you'll need to meet with school officials before the first bell to develop written emergency treatment plans and make lifesaving preparations. As the parent of an allergic child, you must be the guide for teachers, administrators, cafeteria workers, and support staff. Clear communication and a cooperative spirit are the most important tools you'll need to work with the school in keeping your child safe.

As nut and peanut allergies among children become more common, it's more and more likely that your school will have already had some experience in dealing with these allergies. If so, the administration may already have established procedures to handle the problem, and staff may have already been trained to handle a severe allergic reaction. Even if the school has not had any nut-allergic pupils before, however, staff and administrators will almost certainly be aware of the problem. The vast majority of allergic children do very well in mainstream schools thanks to good communication between parents, schools, teachers, doctors, and education authorities.

The key factor in minimizing the risks at school for a child who is allergic to nuts or peanuts is to make sure that as many people as possible—both teachers and students—know about the allergy. In some schools, photographs of severely allergic students are posted in the teachers' lounge for just this reason. Some schools also routinely train teachers to administer an EpiPen.

Making Schools Safe for Kids

You may be surprised to learn that your child's school has already taken steps to prevent allergic reactions to nuts or peanuts, even if none of their students are currently allergic. Many schools have adopted policies restricting the presence of nuts on the school grounds. For example, in many schools nuts are no longer used as an ingredient in prepared lunches, because of the cross-contamination potential. Some schools extend this ban on nuts to include snacks or packed lunches brought from home.

How to Talk to Your School About Nut Allergies

Ideally, parents, the school, and the allergic child should all work together to create a plan for managing the child's nut or peanut allergy. Before school starts in the fall, schedule visits with school staff to discuss your child's food allergy. Meet with the principal, teachers, counselor, nurse, and cafeteria personnel to share information and provide feedback. Be positive and encourage questions, and ask for copies of any forms you'll need so that your child can have an EpiPen at school. Don't forget to ask about the use of nuts or peanuts in arts and crafts classes or science activities.

All medications your child needs, along with completed medical forms, should be brought to the meeting. This can be a good time to demonstrate the use of an EpiPen if your child's doctor has prescribed one.

Next, you'll also need to discuss how any potential problems will be handled. All schools have a clear procedure for calling an ambulance in an emergency, but in the unlikely event that your child has a severe allergic reaction, immediate medical treatment will be necessary while waiting for the ambulance to arrive. Try to work with the school to create an emergency response plan should an allergic reaction occur.

Any child allergic to nuts or peanuts should have an EpiPen at school if the child is at risk for an anaphylactic reaction. Some states allow a child to carry the medication with him, but a few still do not. Find out what your state allows, and what your school is prepared to approve. Remember—when it comes to anaphylaxis, seconds count. Make sure that teachers and the school nurse are trained to administer an EpiPen before being faced with the need to use the shot, and that they understand how to recognize the symptoms of an allergic reaction. The school will almost certainly want parents to sign a written agreement giving consent to the staff to administer an EpiPen if necessary.

If your child can carry an EpiPen, stress to your child that this means it should always be in the child's backpack with him in class—not his locker. And even if your child carries an EpiPen, you still should make sure the teacher or the nurse also has a pen. If your child is not allowed to carry an EpiPen, his teacher and the school nurse should always have one within reach.

It's also important to make sure the school understands that the child's medication must be taken along on any school trips. While teachers will usually remember that an EpiPen must be taken along, it's a good idea to remind your child's teacher by writing a note directly on the parent permission slip. In addition, you may want to remind the teacher again on the day of the outing.

During your meeting with the school, you may find that some teachers may not feel comfortable having a severely allergic child in their class. If this is the case, it's better to be honest about it up front. You and your child will feel much more comfortable in a classroom where the teacher has the ability to respond to an emergency properly.

Day Care and Preschool

Any child's first day in day care or preschool can be fraught with anxiety for the parents, but this can be even more worrisome for children with a nut allergy. The extent to which the allergy will be a problem at a preschool or day care will depend on the kind of activities in the daily routine, but in any case you'll need to discuss the situation with staff.

The kind of snacks offered to children in day care or preschool vary. Some schools may offer fruit, cookies, or sandwiches; children who stay for a full day at preschool may eat several snacks and meals throughout the day.

Even if your child isn't going to eat any meals at day care or preschool, you can count on the fact that some kind of snack will be offered. If your child has suffered any severe reaction to nuts or peanuts in the past, the day care or preschool will need to have an EpiPen available should a reaction occur while the child is in their care.

In some cases you may want to provide food from home for your child, unless you have checked out the foods offered to the children and you feel satisfied that they are safe. It's also worth making sure that your child won't come into contact with any nuts in any of the activities.

If parents have prepared them carefully, children with nut allergies often have a very mature approach to eating at a very young age. As long as they have something special to eat, they probably won't be upset that it's not exactly the same thing that the others are eating.

If the child has ever had a severe reaction to nuts or peanuts, an EpiPen must be kept at the day care center or preschool. Everyone on staff should be aware of the condition, be able to recognize the symptoms of an allergic reaction, and understand what to do if the child has an allergic reaction. In addition, it's a good idea to write down a detailed list of procedures to follow in the event of a severe allergic reaction, to be kept in the office with emergency contact phone numbers. The day care center or preschool will almost certainly want some kind of formal written agreement signed by the parents to give permission for medication to be administered to the child if necessary.

Classroom Policies

Once you're sure the prospective teacher is willing to handle the added responsibility of having an allergic child in the class, you should discuss classroom policies. Parents should provide written information on the child's condition and needs to that year's teacher (a new letter should then be presented to each new teacher as the child progresses through the grades). You'll need to explain that because it's normal for kids to want to share their lunchbox treats with their friends, the teacher (or the school) needs to establish a rule prohibiting lunchbox sharing—if there isn't already a rule in place. (More and more schools are establishing these rules.)

Many teachers (especially in lower grades) like to offer snacks or treats as rewards to their students, which may pose a problem for the nut-allergic child.

Since highly processed foods are more likely to contain peanut products, talk to your child's teacher about offering simple snacks such as raw vegetables or fruit instead. Even better, try to encourage teachers to offer non-food rewards or prizes, such as stickers, pencils, erasers, or collector cards, so that no child is left out when it comes to a reward.

School Lunch Policies

Next, it's important to discuss with the administration your child's individual meal requirements and how school lunches can be kept as safe as possible. Most public schools hire their own cooks and kitchen staff, but if the school's kitchen staff is hired by an outside catering group, you'll need to make sure the catering supervisor is fully aware of your child's particular requirements.

Since many children allergic to nuts or peanuts can be affected by the slightest whiff of nut dust, many schools have set up a "nut-free" table for nut-allergic children; the child's friends are free to sit there as well, as long as no nuts are contained in the meals brought from home. Many other schools simply ban nuts in any form in prepared school lunches; some go so far as to ban peanuts and nuts in lunches children bring from home.

Unexpected Situations

No matter how carefully you plan, unexpected occasions arise when food is offered, such as at birthdays, winter holidays, spring holidays, school parties, and school outings. Any of these situations may include food that is different from what is normally offered in the school lunchroom. Even if a nut-allergic child is bringing food from home for lunches and breaks, these special situations can pose uncertainties both for your child and the teachers.

Parents might suggest to the teacher that a box of nut-free treats be kept at the school as a good way of coping with any of these unexpected situations. This way, the child won't miss out on eating something special without being exposed to potential risks from unfamiliar foods.

Letter to Classmates

Some parents choose to ask their child's school to mail a letter to the parents of each child who will be in the classroom with an allergic student, explaining the nature of the child's nut or peanut allergy, and asking that no nuts, peanuts, or products made with nuts or peanuts be included in food sent to school for bake sales, class parties, snacks, or lunches. Since some parents may not understand the real physical risks imposed by inadvertently eating nuts, if you're going to send a letter it's a good idea to be quite specific:

Dear Parent:

One of the students in your child's class this year has a life-threatening allergy to nuts and peanuts. This means that nuts and peanuts, or foods with even the slightest trace of nuts and peanuts or nut or peanut oil, may cause a severe reaction that can result in death within minutes. For this reason, we are asking that you not send any food containing nuts or peanuts to school with your child this year. Be sure to check the ingredients of all foods your children bring to school. (Coconut is not a nut and does not pose any risk.)

Eating nuts or peanuts in any form—even inhaling nut dust—could be fatal to a child who is allergic to these foods. It's a good idea to read food labels of any items you're thinking of sending in to class, since nut and peanut products are used in a variety of foods, candy, and pastries.

Many parents may not realize the problem of hidden nuts (for example, many parents may not realize that marzipan contains almonds). For this reason, you may want to consider including in your letter a list of nut-containing products to help parents remember (see Chapter 5). It's usually a good idea to send additional reminders home every other month or so throughout the school year, because many parents, despite good intentions, often forget that certain food snacks can be dangerous. A brief reminder can prevent a serious reaction during a class party.

However, some experts don't believe that sending a letter to your child's classmates is a good idea. Some parents prefer not to rely on other students' parents to check foods for nuts, but believe that the safest policy is to have the allergic student eat only snacks brought from home. In some cases, the student's parents choose to be responsible for purchasing snacks for the entire class, so they can be sure the food is safe. I usually advise parents that whether or not they send a letter is up to them and that they should do whatever makes them feel most comfortable.

In any case, you may find it helpful to attend all class parties so you can help monitor the nut situation—especially in lower grades where your allergic child may still not be fully aware of the dangers of hidden nuts. You also may want to attend any field trips where the child leaves the school grounds. On the other hand, many working parents these days can't take time off to attend all trips and parties. In this case, you can call the class parent or teaching assistant and ask for help in monitoring the situation. If your child's school doesn't have "class parents," you can ask a friend with a child in the same class to monitor your child.

The First Day of Class

A child with severe food allergies may be uncomfortable with being labeled a "problem child" and may worry about being teased. To forestall such problems, the teacher should explain the child's allergy to the class on the first day in a warm, supportive, and understated way. If the fact of the allergy is presented calmly and kindly, classmates usually become quite vigilant and help watch out for nuts or peanuts in food products to protect their friend.

From a very young age, children with these allergies can be taught to protect themselves. For example, they should be trained from a very early age to only eat food from their own lunch box. You may want to consider giving your allergic child an alarm or whistle that can be triggered in the event of a reaction on the playground. Be sure to tell the teacher about the device and what it means—and impress on your child never to use it unless there's a true emergency.

Talking to Your Allergic Child

Children who are at risk of severe allergic reactions are usually quite normal in every respect, until they come into contact with nuts or peanuts. It's important to allow your child to develop normally, and to try hard not to make him feel different from his classmates. It's also important to reassure your child that prompt and efficient action will be taken should an allergic reaction occur. Although you and your child have a right to confidentiality, you should consider the benefits of an open management policy. As with any other medical condition, privacy and the need for prompt and effective care should be balanced with sensitivity. This is especially true with nut and peanut allergies, when the more people at school who understand the problem, the better.

By following all these guidelines, your child should be well on the way to a happy, healthy school year.

In the Next Chapter

Now that you've learned what nut and peanut allergies are and how they are diagnosed, treated, and managed, it's time to learn what scientists are planning when it comes to the future management of nut allergies.

9

In the Future

No matter how good you are at staying away from nuts or peanuts, avoidance is not a complete solution to the problem. Researchers are currently working on a wide variety of strategies to lessen the impact of these allergies. Some scientists are studying ways to make peanuts and nuts allergy-free, while others are trying to come up with vaccines to lessen the severity of reactions or eradicate them altogether.

In one of the most exciting developments in allergy research, scientists have for the first time developed an experimental drug that could protect people from potentially deadly allergic reactions after accidentally eating peanuts. News of a possible vaccine that could help most people with peanut allergies avoid life-threatening allergic reactions flashed around the world after a report was published in the March 14, 2003, issue of the *New England Journal of Medicine*. It's not a perfect solution—patients would need lifelong monthly shots of the drug (called TNX-901), and still would have to guard against eating peanuts. But while the monthly shots aren't a cure, the drug should let these people avoid severe complications if they unknowingly eat one or two peanuts—which is typically how people are exposed.

The report described a genetically engineered, altered form of peanut protein that may have potential as a vaccine against peanut sensitivity, according to a research team led by Donald Leung, M.D., Ph.D., of the National Jewish Medical and Research Center, and Hugh Sampson, M.D., of Mount Sinai School of Medicine. The team found that treatment with an anti–IgE antibody raised the average level at which study participants began reacting to peanuts from about half a peanut to almost nine peanuts. Researchers estimate that most of the 50 to 100 annual fatal reactions to peanuts occur after an allergic person accidentally eats the equivalent of just one to two nuts. The researchers also presented their findings March 10, 2003, in Denver at the annual meeting of the American Academy of Allergy, Asthma, and Immunology.

In the study, eighty-two people with immediate allergic reactions to peanuts got monthly shots of either a placebo or TNX-901 for four months. There were three different doses of TNX-901; neither doctors nor patients knew who got what. Those on the highest dose could handle an average of almost nine peanuts' worth of peanut flour at the end, compared with about a half-peanut at the start.

IgE is the molecule that binds to a group of cells called mast cells, which then triggers the allergic response. TNX-901, the treatment used in this study, is a genetically engineered antibody made by Tanox Incorporated that binds to the IgE molecule and prevents it from triggering the allergic response.

The study results indicate that the anti–IgE antibody could become the first preventive medicine for peanut allergies. If future studies bear out this initial promise, anti–IgE could not only save lives, but help lift the cloud of fear that people with peanut allergies live under every time they eat.

Each year, thousands of people rush to hospital emergency rooms after accidentally ingesting peanuts or nuts. Up to now, strict avoidance has been the only way to prevent an allergic reaction. But avoiding all exposure to peanuts can be impossible, especially since food labels don't always mention tiny amounts of peanuts that are found in some foods.

An earlier study had reported that fatal reactions occurred after a patient ate a tuna sandwich made with a knife that had not been thoroughly cleaned after spreading peanut butter, or eating cookies that had been made on factory equipment earlier used to make peanut-filled cookies. Existing medications, including epinephrine, antihistamines, and bronchodilators, are taken only after the peanuts have been eaten and are not always effective.

Researchers caution that anti-IgE therapy is not a cure for peanut allergy. Patients would probably have to continue the injections for the benefits to continue, and they still would need to be careful about what they eat. But because they could consume many more peanuts or nuts without serious reaction, the fear of accidental ingestion (which is what detracts most from quality of life for many patients) would be eliminated.

Blocking IgE is considered a major advance because it inhibits the allergic response at an earlier stage than other medicines, effectively stopping it before it begins. A slightly different anti–IgE molecule has shown promise in treating severe hay fever and asthma.

In the study, which was randomized, double-blind, and placebo-controlled, eighty-two people ages twelve to sixty with severe peanut allergy were given four injections at monthly intervals of either a placebo or one of three doses (150 mg, 300 mg, or 450 mg) of TNX-901. Before the trial began, researchers established each patient's sensitivity to increasing doses of peanut flour.

Blood levels of IgE were measured before the injections began and periodically measured again throughout the test. Two to four weeks after the final injection, patients underwent one more food challenge with peanut flour.

Researchers found that the larger the dose of TNX-901, the less sensitive patients became to peanuts. Nearly a quarter of the patients receiving the highest dose of TNX-901 consumed about twenty-four peanuts with no reaction. Many patients still reacted to peanuts even after the injections, but on average, they could eat more peanuts without a reaction, and reacted less vigorously to the peanuts they did eat.

Unfortunately, the drug will not be available for another few years. Although TNX-901 is on the fast track for federal approval, its critical third round of tests has been stalled by legal disagreements among the three companies owning its rights—Genentech, Tanox Incorporated, and Novartis Pharmaceuticals. Once those tests start, it will probably take three to four years before the U.S. Food and Drug Administration approves the drug.

Hypoallergenic Nuts

Because nut and peanut derivatives are extremely common substances used as protein extenders in many foods, and are often a hidden component of processed foods, some scientists are trying to make a hypoallergenic nut. Researchers at the University of Arkansas

Medical School in Little Rock are working to develop allergy-free peanuts through genetic engineering.

Before developing such products, scientists must first identify the specific proteins that are responsible for triggering the allergic response. So far, a number of the proteins responsible for peanut or nut allergy have been identified.

Modified Peanut Protein Vaccine

In research to develop a vaccine against peanut allergy, the major peanut proteins are modified so that they do not bind with IgE immunoglobulins, but still stimulate an immune response. This would block a reaction if an unmodified peanut protein was eaten at a later date. To test it, researchers created peanut allergies in mice and then gave them doses of the new vaccine. The mice that had not received the vaccine experienced trouble breathing, while those that had were fine. Scientists are hoping to get FDA approval to test the vaccine in humans soon.

DNA Vaccines

In one study, researchers found that when mice were given oral doses of the gene that directs production of one of the major peanut protein allergens, the gene began to function within the cells of the mouse's gut.

These mice showed a reduction in the development of anaphylaxis to peanuts.

Anti-IgE Vaccine

This medication was developed for the treatment of asthma and allergic rhinitis, and now may find a new use in preventing anaphylaxis. This vaccine may be capable of reducing the severity of an anaphylactic reaction by blocking IgE.

Helpful Bacteria

Certain helpful bacteria (such as lactobacillus) that do not cause infection in humans may provide some protection against the development of allergy.

Until Then

Although medical treatments to desensitize or minimize peanut and other food allergy reactions are being developed, they still won't be widely available for several years. Until then, I tell my patients that avoiding nuts or peanuts is the best way to prevent allergic reactions.

Appendix

International Health Insurance Companies

Access America, Inc.
Richmond, VA
(866) 807-3982 or (800) 284-8300
www.worldaccess.com

AIGAssist
American International Group, Inc.
New York, NY
(800) 382-6986
www.aandh.aig.com
www.resultsources.com

ASA, Inc.
(international insurance consultants)
Phoenix, AZ
(888) ASA-8288
www.asaincor.com

AXA Assistance
Bethesda, MD
(301) 214-8200
www.axa-assistance-usa.com

Clements International
Washington, DC
(800) 872-0067
www.clements.com

CSA Travel Protection
San Diego, CA
(888) 873-5484
www.csatravelprotection.com

Gateway
Seabury & Smith
Washington, DC
(800) 282-4495
e-mail: gateway.dc@seabury.com

Health Care Global
(also known as Medhelp or Wallach & Company
or Healthcare Abroad)
Middleburg, VA
(800) 237-6615

Highway to Health, Inc.
Fairfax, VA
(703) 322-1515
(Also provides destination-based travel health information for cities worldwide.)

International Medical Group (IMG)
Indianapolis, IN
(800) 628-4664

MultiNational Underwriters
Indianapolis, IN
(800) 605-2282
e-mail: insurance@mnui.com

Mutual of Omaha
Tele-Trip Company
Omaha, NE
(800) 228-9792

Petersen International Underwriters, Inc.
Valencia, CA
(800) 345-8816
e-mail: piu@piu.org

Travelex
Omaha, NE
(800) 228-9792

Travel Guard International
Stevens Point, WI
(800) 826-1300

Travel Insurance Services
InterMedical Division
Walnut Creek, CA
(800) 937-1387

TripGuard Plus
Northridge, CA
(800) 423-3632

Unicard Travel Association
Overland Park, KS
(800) 501-0352

Universal Service and Assistance
Alexandria, VA
(800) 770-9111

Well on the Road
Sunnyvale, CA
www.wellontheroad.com

Worldwide Assistance
Washington, DC
(800) 777-8710 ext. 417

Glossary

Adrenalin: The trade name for a drug (epinephrine) used to treat severe allergies.

adrenaline: The generic name for Adrenalin, also known as epinephrine.

allergen: Substance that triggers an allergic reaction by inducing the formation of immunoglobulin E (IgE).

allergist: A physician who specializes in the treatment of allergies.

allergy: An inappropriate response of the immune system to a substance that should normally be harmless and induce no symptoms.

anaphylaxis: The sudden, potentially fatal reaction triggered by an allergy; it includes symptoms such as swelling of the lips and face, breathing problems, hives, a drop in blood pressure, vomiting, and diarrhea.

antibody: A protein produced by white blood cells to destroy a substance perceived by the immune system as "foreign."

antigen: A substance that can trigger an allergic reaction, which produces antibodies as part of the immune system's response to infection or disease. An allergen is a type of antigen that evokes an IgE antibody response.

antihistamine: A drug that blocks the action of histamine, a substance produced by the immune system during an allergic reaction.

asthma: A chronic inflammatory lung disorder that causes attacks of breathing problems ranging from wheezing to airway obstruction.

atopy: An IgE-linked anaphylactic response that is usually genetically determined.

eczema: An inflammatory skin condition that causes lesions, itching, and scaly blisters.

enzyme: A protein that causes a chemical reaction in the body.

epinephrine: A hormone produced naturally in the body that is responsible for the body's "fight or flight" response. Also known as *adrenaline*.

EpiPen: A spring-loaded syringe that has been preloaded with epinephrine.

food allergen: A food protein that isn't broken down in cooking or by stomach acids, and that may cause an allergic reaction.

food intolerance: A general term describing an abnormal physiological response to a food or food component. This reaction does not involve the immune system.

food allergy: An immunologic reaction (usually IgE-related) linked to eating a food or food additive, and in some cases skin contact or inhalation of a food or food additive.

histamine: A chemical found throughout the body that is released during an allergic reaction. Histamine is one substance responsible for many of the symptoms of an allergic attack, including hives, itchy skin, and narrowing of the bronchial tubes and airways in the lungs.

hives: An allergic reaction in the skin that causes itchy, raised white bumps surrounded by inflammation. Hives are known medically as *urticaria*.

IgE: See *immunoglobulin E*.

immune system: The united efforts of cells and proteins in the body that protect against harmful viruses and bacteria. The immune system also plays an important role in the development of allergies and the subsequent reaction to allergic substances.

immunogen: Any substance that can induce an immune response.

immunoglobulin E (IgE): An antibody that circulates through the blood that is created to protect the body from infection. IgE attaches to mast cells in the respiratory and intestinal tracts and may cause allergic reactions.

immunoglobulins: A general term for antibodies produced by the immune system that bind to substances recognized as "foreign." Immunoglobulins sometimes bind to harmless antigens and provoke an allergic reaction.

mast cell: A type of cell that produces and stores histamine. Mast cells are found throughout the body. During an allergic reaction, an allergen stimulates the release of antibodies that attach themselves to mast cells and trigger the release of histamine.

RAST: A blood test (radioallergosorbent test) that measures specific IgE.

Resources

Associations

Allergy and Asthma Network
2751 Prosperity Avenue, Suite 150
Fairfax, VA 22031
(800) 878-4403
www.aanma.org

Founded in 1985, AANMA is a national nonprofit network of families whose desire is to overcome allergies and asthma. AANMA produces the most accurate, timely, practical, and livable alternatives to allergy problems.

American Academy of Allergy, Asthma, and Immunology
611 East Wells Street
Milwaukee, WI 53202
(414) 272-6071; (800) 822-2762
e-mail: info@aaaai.org
www.aaaai.org

A driving force in the study and treatment of allergic diseases through education, research, and cooperation since 1943, the Academy offers lots of up-to-date information. This large professional medical specialty organization represents allergists, clinical immunologists, allied health professionals, and other physicians with a special interest in allergy.

American Academy of Pediatrics (AAP)
141 Northwest Point Boulevard
Elk Grove Village, IL 60007-1098
(847) 434-4000
www.aap.org

The AAP is committed to the health and well-being of infants, adolescents, and young adults. The website offers news articles and tips on health for families.

American College of Allergy, Asthma, and Immunology
85 West Algonquin Road, Suite 550
Arlington Heights, IL 60005
http://allergy.mcg.edu

An organization of allergists/immunologists and health professionals dedicated to quality patient care.

American Peanut Council
1500 King Street, Suite 301
Alexandria, VA 22314
www.peanutsusa.com

The American Peanut Council serves as a forum for all segments of the peanut industry to discuss issues that impact the production, utilization, and marketing of peanuts and peanut products worldwide, including peanut allergies.

Anaphylaxis Canada
416 Moore Avenue, Suite 306
Toronto, ON M4G 1C9
(416) 785-5666
www.anaphylaxis.org

Anaphylaxis Canada's mission is to inform, support, educate, and advocate for the needs of individuals and families living with anaphylaxis and to conduct and support research related to anaphylaxis.

Asthma and Allergy Foundation of America (AAFA)
1233 20th Street NW, Suite 402
Washington, DC 20036
(202) 466-7643
www.aafa.org

A nonprofit patient organization dedicated to improving the quality of life for people with

asthma and allergies and their caregivers,
through education, advocacy, and research.
AAFA, founded in 1953, provides practical
information, community-based services, support,
and referrals through a national network of
chapters and educational support groups. AAFA
also sponsors research toward better treatments
and a cure for asthma and allergic diseases.

**Food Allergy and Anaphylaxis Network
(FAAN)**
10400 Eaton Place, Suite 107
Fairfax, VA 22030-2208
(703) 691-3179
www.foodallergy.org
    FAAN was established in 1991 and has more
than 25,000 members worldwide, including
families, dietitians, nurses, physicians, school
staff, representatives from government agencies,
and the food and pharmaceutical industries.

**Food Allergy Research and Resource
Program**
143 H. C. Filley Hall
University of Nebraska
Lincoln, NE 68583-0919
(402) 472-4430
www.farrp.org

FARRP's primary goal is to "help the food industry address one of its most daunting challenges—allergies." FARRP membership is open to food processors, food manufacturers, ingredient manufacturers, equipment manufacturers, and other companies involved in the food processing industry.

Joint Council of Allergy, Asthma, and Immunology
50 North Brockway, Suite 33
Palatine, IL 60067
(847) 934-1918
www.jcaai.org

JCAAI represents allergy and immunology specialists in federal and state regulatory and governmental agencies, in Congress, in areas of reimbursement, and in other socioeconomic areas where appropriate. JCAAI serves as a single voice in these areas representing the specialty of allergy/immunology; it represents approximately 4,200 allergists.

MedicAlert Foundation
2323 Colorado Ave.
Turlock, CA 95382
(800) 432-5378
www.medicalert.org

MedicAlert Foundation is one of the world's largest nonprofit membership organizations with one mission—to protect and save lives. The foundation provides emergency medical information about members having a medical emergency to authorized medical professionals. MedicAlert Foundation protects the privacy and confidentiality of members by never releasing information to unauthorized personnel or organizations.

National Institute of Allergy and Infectious Diseases
Building 31, Room 7A-50
31 Center Drive, MSC 2520
Bethesda, MD 20892
(301) 496-5717
www.niaid.nih.gov

NIAID is a component of the National Institutes of Health (NIH), and conducts and supports research that strives to understand, treat, and ultimately prevent the myriad infectious, immunologic, and allergic diseases that threaten hundreds of millions of people worldwide.

Websites

Allergic Child
www.allergicchild.com

Informative site regarding children with various and multiple food allergies (nuts, peanuts, dairy, shellfish, soy, and many others). Discusses many subjects that affect parents and children with these allergies, such as buying foods, reading labels, and traveling.

Allergy, Asthma, and Immunology Online
http://allergy.mcg.edu

Website providing information on a wide variety of allergies and asthma problems.

Anaphylaxis Canada
www.anaphylaxis.org

DietaryCard.Com
www.dietarycard.com

This company provides online service for translation cards for people with all types of nut allergies, with custom-made explanations. Cards are available in Spanish, French, Italian, German, and English, and cost $7 each or $21 for all five.

Food Anaphylaxis Education
www.faemi.org

Mothers of Children Having Allergies
www.mochallergies.org

No Nuts for Me
www.nonutsforme.com
   Interactive website to educate about nut allergies.

Peanut Allergy
http://allergies.about.com/cs/peanuts
   Collection of some articles and links regarding peanut allergies.

PeanutAllergy.com
www.peanutallergy.com
   Information, links, discussion board, and more regarding peanut allergies. Site also includes a membership.

Index